A LOVE THAT NO LONGER EXIST

TALEAH STEPHENSON

Copyright Notice
© 2024 Taleah Stephenson. All rights reserved.
No part of this book may be reproduced, distributed, or transmitted in any form or by any means, including photocopying, recording, or other electronic or mechanical methods, without the prior written permission of the author, except in the case of brief quotations used in reviews or articles. For permission requests, please contact ta.author25@gmail.com.

DEAR READERS,

IS LOVE WORTH RISKING IT ALL?

**THROUGHOUT ALL THE HEARTBREAK WE EXPERIENCE,
IT'S NOTHING QUITE LIKE THE FIRST ONE.**

MY HEART FEELS DEFEATED.
DESTROYING THE MANY BARRIERS WE HAVE TO PROTECT US —
IT WASN'T ENOUGH.
WE'VE BEEN DEFEATED
BY THIS SO-CALLED
"LOVE".

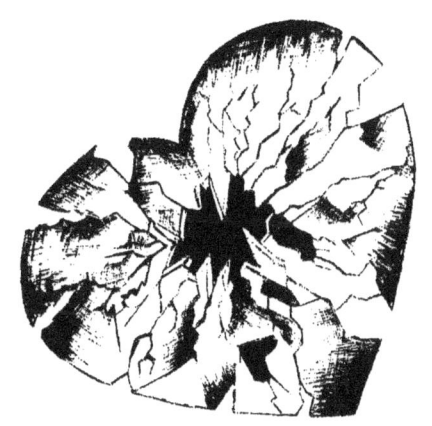

IT ALWAYS END THE SAME WAY—
A GIRL,
BROKEN HEARTED,
ALL ALONE,
WISHING FOR SOMEONE TO CHOOSE HER.
BUT ALL THEY DID WAS BREAK HER,
A GIRL THAT WILL NEVER BE CHOSEN.

IT'S DRIVING ME CRAZY NOT HEARING FROM YOU,
CONSTANTLY WONDERING IF YOUR THINKING ABOUT ME—
OR AM I STILL JUST CRAZY OVER YOU?

WHY DID WE HAVE TO PLAY THIS CHILDISH GAME,
TO SEE WHO'S GOING TO REACH OUT TO WHO ?
A SILLY GAME SOCIAL MEDIA MADE:
"NO CONTACT".

I THOUGHT SENDING YOU A MESSAGE WOULD CHANGE HOW I FELT —
TO SEE IF I'M REALLY A GHOST OF YOUR PAST —
BUT IT MADE ME ACCEPT WHAT HAS ACTUALLY HAPPENED.

I DON'T REGRET IT, BECAUSE I NEEDED IT.
I NEEDED TO SEE THAT IT WAS NO GOING BACK,
TO KNOW WE LOST HOPE OF OUR LOVE .
HOPING YOU'D RESPOND,
BUT HOPING YOU DON'T TEXT BACK.
TO NOT CARE IF YOU SEEN IT ,
NOT CARE IF YOU RESPONDED,
BUT FINALLY ACCEPTING HOW I FELT.
REALIZING, AFTER EVERYTHING,
I STILL WANT TO BE KEPT.

I STILL CARE FOR YOU,
BUT NOT FOR WHAT YOU PUT ME THROUGH.

I'M WILLING TO LET SOMEONE IN,
BUT NOT LIKE I WAS WILLING TO LET YOU.
YOU'VE MADE ME SCARED TO EVEN LET SOMEONE FEEL ME—
THE WARM EMBRACE YOU ONCE NEEDED,
THE EMBRACE I ONCE BEGGED FOR.
MAYBE I JUST NEED A HUG.

A HUG SO EMOTIONALLY CONNECTED YOU TAKE MY PAIN AWAY—
A HUG SO CONNECTED, ALL I CAN DO IS CRY.
CRY ABOUT HOW MUCH I'VE BEEN BETRAYED,
WHY I'M SO STUBBORN,
WHY I'M SO INDEPENDENT,
WHY I'M SO IMPATIENT—
BUT WHY AM I SO PATIENT?
NOBODY'S PATIENT WITH ME.
IT'S DO THIS NOW, OR I WON'T DO FOR YOU.
BUT WHEN AM I GOING TO BE ABLE TO TEACH THAT LESSON?

THE LESSON OF CONDITIONS—
BUT WHAT ARE MY CONDITIONS?
BESIDES EMOTIONAL CONDITIONS,
BESIDES THAT HUG I DESCRIBED,
BESIDES THAT CONVERSATION I ONCE WANTED,
BESIDES THE LOVE I ONCE WANTED SO BAD.
I HATED MYSELF FOR IT,
BUT A HUG FROM SOMEONE THAT CAN EASE MY PAIN—
THE PAIN EVERYONE CAUSED ME,
BUT MOST RECENTLY, YOU.

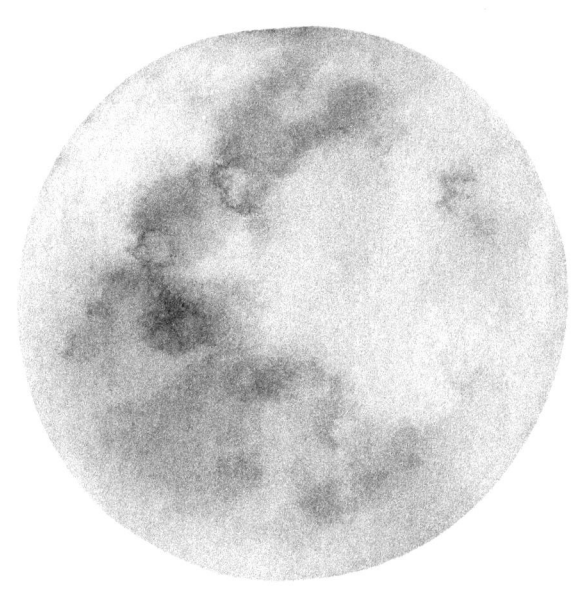

YOU WERE IN MY **DREAM** LAST NIGHT,
I WAS ABLE TO FEEL SOMETHING I MISSED.

I GOT IT WITHOUT NEEDING YOU—
MY HEART ISN'T HEAVY.

I'M OKAY...

IF I STAY LIKE THIS, I'LL BE OKAY.

BEING ABLE TO REMEMBER US WITHOUT YOUR HARSH WORDS
IS SOMETHING I PRAYED FOR.

MY HEART ACHES, FULL OF PAIN—
SADNESS,
DISAPPOINT,
ANGER .
BUT IT'S SCARING ME, BECAUSE IT FEEL LIKE MY ACTUAL HEART HURTS—
LIKE THE BLOOD STARTED TO PUMP SLOWER,
LIKE SOMEBODY'S HOLDING MY HEART AND SQUEEZING IT SO TIGHT,
I CAN BARELY HEAR MY HEARTBEAT.
WHY COULDN'T YOU CARE FOR ME?
IT WAS SO EASY FOR YOU TO MOVE ON.
IT MADE ME HATE YOU
AND SAY, "FUCK HIM,"
BUT THEN I WANTED TO FUCK YOU AND LOVE YOU
ONE LAST TIME—
THE LAST TIME YOU'LL EVER FEEL MY EMBRACE AND MY TOUCH.
THE LAST TIME YOU'LL EVER TASTE ME.

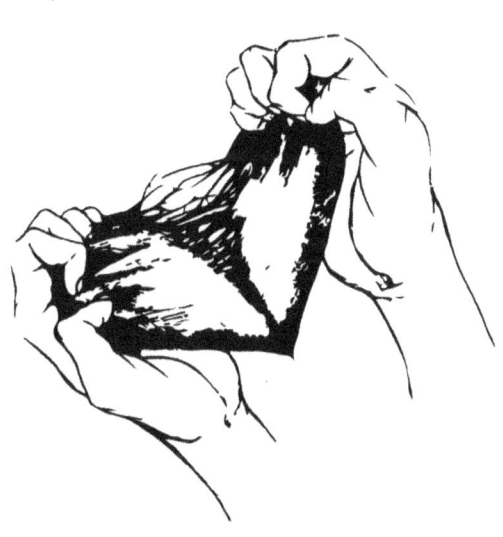

CONTINUED.

I DON'T WANT TO EVER FEEL LIKE THIS AGAIN—
HAVING TO CALL YOU A WHOLE BUNCH OF BITCHES
JUST TO HELP ME FIX THESE STITCHES OVER A HEART I DIDN'T TEAR.
I WOULD'VE NEVER IMAGINED IT WOULD'VE BEEN YOU
татo MAKE ME HATE YOU.

TO MAKE ME HURT SO BAD I CAN PHYSICALLY FEEL IT THROUGH MY CHEST,
WHILE YOUR LIVING YOUR BEST LIFE, TALKING TO GIRLS—
THE GIRLS YOU'VE HAD YOUR EYES ON FOR MONTHS,
THE GIRL YOU BROKE MY HEART TO TOUCH.
IT'LL NEVER MAKE SENSE TO ME,
BUT ALL I KNOW IS I COULD NEVER LOVE YOU THE SAME.

MY HEART WAS SCREAMING AND CRYING FOR YOU,
BUT NOW IT'S SILENT.

WHY CAN'T I HEAR OR FEEL YOU ANYMORE?
HAVE I GIVEN UP ON YOU LIKE YOU GAVE UP ON ME?
SOMETHING MY MIND KNEW,
SOMETHING IT WAS TRYING TO PREVENT.

KNOWING MY BODY STILL LONGS FOR YOU
EVEN AFTER EVERYTHING—
JUST TO BE FELT, RUBBED, AND HELD
THE FEELING I ONLY FEEL WITH YOU.

INTIMACY
WAS A WAY FOR MY HEART TO CONNECT TO YOURS,
BUT I FEEL LIKE YOU GAVE THAT AWAY
THE DAY YOU REJECTED ME.

HOW COULD YOU CONSTANTLY BREAK MY HEART—
A HEART THAT ONLY WANTED AND NEEDED YOU...
UNTIL NOW.

I'M SO AFRAID.
I CAN'T EVEN TELL YOU HOW SCARED I AM—
TO KNOW THE OLD VERSION OF ME HAS VANISHED,
TO KNOW I'M BECOMING SOMEBODY NEW,
THAT YOU'LL NEVER GET THE CHANCE TO KNOW.

I THOUGHT I COULD HANDLE THIS—
SOMETHING I FOUGHT HARD TO FLEE
CAME BACK AND SWEPT ME BACK OFF MY FEET.

NOW I'M FORCING A SMILE,
HOLDING BACK TEARS,
FEELING LIKE SOMETHING JUST SUCKED THE LIFE OUT OF ME.

THINGS I ONCE FOUND JOY IN,
I LOST.
MAYBE THIS HAD NOTHING TO DO WITH YOU.
MAYBE IT HAD SOMETHING TO DO WITH THIS PLAGUE—
THE PLAGUE I HAVE OVER ME AND MY EMOTIONS.

I WANT BETTER FOR ME,
WITH OR WITHOUT YOU—
BUT I JUST WISH IT WAS WITH YOU.

IF I WAS TO GO BACK,
I WOULD MELT IN YOUR ARMS,
FEELING LIKE THE GIRL ON TOP OF THE WORLD.

SADLY, ITS NOT YOUR WORLD—
BECAUSE YOU DON'T HAVE A WORLD TO GIVE,
AT LEAST NOT TO ME.
YOU GAVE ME A WORLD FULL OF LIES,
HOPELESS PROMISES,
AND BROKEN BELIEFS

CONTINUED.

YOU WANTED CHANGE,
BUT WHEN I OFFERED ROOM FOR CHANGE,
I WAS THE ONE TO BLAME.

IF I WAS TO GO BACK,
AM I READY FOR THAT FEELING?
THE FEELING OF FEELING LOVE IN A PHYSICAL WAY,
WHILE MY HEART AND MIND DESIRED IT MENTALLY?

WILL YOU LEARN HOW TO COMPROMISE,
OR WILL YOU CONTINUE TO UNDERMINE WHAT I SAY.

IF I WAS TO GO BACK,
AM I READY FOR THE INSECURITIES THAT PLAGUE A MAN—
TO BRING DOWN A GIRL THAT BROUGHT HERSELF UP?
SOMEONE THAT'S NOT MAN ENOUGH…
A BOY IN A YOUNG MAN'S BODY.

NO, I CAN'T GO BACK.
I WOULD LOVE TO, BUT THERE'S NO MORE LOVE THERE—
AT LEAST, NOT ENOUGH FOR ME.

I KNOW WHAT YOU COULD OFFER,
BUT I OFFERED MYSELF MORE.
SO NOW THE BARE MINIMUM WAS IN HELL,
BUT IN HEAVEN, IT WAS FOR YOU,
BY CLOUDING MY MIND AND MAKING EVERYTHING JUST FINE.

THAT'S WHY I CAN'T GO BACK.
I DON'T WANT YOU TO DISTRACT ME
AND BECOME MY EVERYTHING—
SOMETHING I AM NOT TO YOU.
EVERYTHING.
I'M JUST ANOTHER PIECE OF MEAT
YOU SPENT TIME WITH, CRIED WITH,
HELPED LOVE, BUILD, AND DESTROY ALL IN ONE.
YET, YOU GO BACK TO THE ONES THAT DESTROYED YOU MOST.

I'M CONSTANTLY TRYING TO FIX A BROKEN HEART I DIDN'T EVEN BREAK,
AS YOU TAKE YOUR PAIN OUT ON ME.
I CAN'T GO BACK .
I NEED TO STAY WHERE I'M AT—

NO LONGER WORRYING ABOUT YOU LEAVING ONE MORNING.
MY HEARTS IS HEALING AGAIN.
I'M FEELING A CALMING SENSATION WHEN I THINK OF YOU AND US.
I FEEL LIKE I CAN BREATH ALL OVER AGAIN—
AND THE "AGAIN" IS NOT BECAUSE OF YOU .

SO WHY WOULD I GO BACK?
TO SOMEONE THAT MADE ME CRY,
THE REASON WHY I COULDN'T EAT OR DRINK?

SOMEONE THAT GAVE ME BROKEN PROMISES—
PROMISES I KNEW NOT TO BELIEVE.
BUT HERE I AM BEING A HOPELESS ROMANTIC,
GIVING YOU EVERYTHING
WHEN I GOT NOTHING IN RETURN—
BESIDES A BROKEN HEART AND CONFUSED MIND.
WHICH IS WHY, IF I WAS TO EVER GO BACK,
I KNOW I COULDN'T.

AFTER ALL, I CAN'T STOP HOW YOU TREAT ME,
BUT I CHANGE YOUR ACCESS TO ME.

TIT FOR TAT IS A DANGEROUS GAME TO PLAY—
A GAME THAT CAN LEAVE ME AND YOU BOTH BROKEN,
WONDERING, *HOW DID WE GET HERE?*

IT'S ALL FOR THE OTHER TO ENDURE THE PAIN OF BEING BROKENHEARTED,
SUCH A FEELING WE WOULDN'T WANT TO GO THROUGH AGAIN—
BUT WOULDN'T MIND PUTTING EACH OTHER THROUGH.

IS THIS THE DEFINITION OF LOVE, TRULY?
WHERE YOU GO THROUGH HELL AND BACK FOR IT?
I DON'T THINK THAT'S LOVE ....
LOVE SHOULD FEEL HEAVENLY AND ANGELIC,
WITH GOD IN THE MIDDLE OF IT—
A BLESSING TO US BOTH,
SO MUCH THAT OUR LOVE NEVER DIES.
BUT SOMETIMES THAT GOOD MOMENT CAN BE SENT FROM THE DEVIL,
DISGUISED AS AN ANGEL TO DISTRACT YOU FROM THE REAL PURPOSE.

SO WHY PLAY TIT FOR TAT WITH THE PERSON YOU LOVE,
WHEN WE'RE FIGHTING FOR THE SAME THING?
WHY HURT THE PERSON YOU'RE SUPPOSED TO LOVE,
TRYING TO PROVE A POINT—
A POINT THAT GETS LOST WITHIN YOUR ACTIONS?

NOW WE'RE ALL BENT OUT OF SHAPE,
ATTEMPTING TO MOLD US BACK TOGETHER,
NO LONGER ABLE TO BLAME EACH OTHER
FROM SOMETHING WE COULD'VE PREVENTED
BY JUST COMMUNICATING WITH EACH OTHER.

BUT WE HAD TO GO TIT FOR TAT,
DOING THINGS WE KNOW IS WRONG,
THAT WE KNOW WILL HURT EACH OTHER,
PLANNING OUR GET BACK.

LET'S PLAY TIT FOR TAT.

IN THAT MOMENT, I KNEW IT WASN'T THERE ANYMORE—
THE SPARK THAT I ONCE CRIED PLENTY OF NIGHTS OVER
WENT OUT ...
DID THE TEARS THAT FELL, CAUSED BY YOU, EXTINGUISH THE SPARK—
OUR SPARK—
OR WAS IT THE MARKS THAT YOU LEFT IN MY HEART?

MY HEART STINGS,
MY BODY ACHES
AT THE LOSE OF FALLING OUT OF LOVE WITH YOU.
THE DESIRE TO KISS YOU IS GONE.
TO BE HELD IS GONE.

I NO LONGER COUNT DOWN THE MINUTES,
EVEN SECONDS, WAITING FOR YOU ANYMORE.
THE FEELINGS BEHIND US ARE FINALLY GONE.

I STARTED TO SHUT YOU OUT,
STOPPED COMMUNICATING THE THINGS THAT BOTHERED ME,
STOPPED CARING,
NO LONGER FEELING THE URGE TO TALK IT OUT.
NO MORE FIGHTING TO BE UNDERSTOOD.

THE REALIZATION CLICKED TO ME
AND BROKE MY HEART EVEN MORE.
IT'S NOT ME WANTING YOU,
IT'S MY HEART CRYING OUT TO YOU.
IT'S MY SOUL BEING ATTRACTED TO THE THING THAT'S DRAINED ME—
MY SOUL WANTING TO GRAB BACK WHAT YOURS TOOK,
WHAT YOURS THRIVED ON.
IT BROKE ME EVEN MORE, KNOWING IT'S DEEPER THEN SKIN,
DEEPER THAN MY HEART, BUT A SPIRITUAL CONNECTION—
A CONNECTION SO DEEP,
I DON'T KNOW IF I COULD BREAK IT.

DO YOU EVEN LOVE ME ?
IS A QUESTION I'VE BEEN ASKING MYSELF LATELY.
HOW CAN YOU TREAT SOMEBODY YOU WANT TO GIVE THE WORLD TO,
LIKE A REGULAR PERSON?

THIS WAS ALL FOR NOTHING.
I PLAYED THE LONG GAME,
THE TEACHING GAME,
THE LOOK-THE-OTHER-WAY GAME.
EVERY TIME I CHOSE YOU, I DIDN'T CHOOSE ME.
EVERY TIME I OVERLOOKED A FLAW, I IGNORED THE FLASHING CAUTION SIGN.
EVERY TIME I REPEATED MYSELF ABOUT SOMETHING THAT HURT ME,
I LOST APART OF ME.

HOW COULD YOU HAVE LOVED ME?
HOW COULD YOU LOVE ME AND I DIDN'T LOVE ME?
YOU COULDN'T.

I HAD TO REALIZE THAT ON MY OWN.
HOW COULD YOU RESPECT ME WHEN I COULDN'T FOR MYSELF?

NOW THAT'S ALL CHANGED.
I'VE TOOK THIS TIME TO CATER TO THE LITTLE GIRL INSIDE ME,
GIVING HER ALL THE INTERNAL HUGS SHE NEEDS ,
THE "I'M HERE FOR YOU"S,
THE "IT'S GOING TO BE OKAY" AND "I'M PROUD OF YOU"S,
THE "YOU CAN GET WHATEVER YOU WANT"S,
ALL WHILE TAKING CARE OF THE OLDER ME,
CATERING TO ME AND WHAT I WANTED YOU TO DO FOR ME.
I USED TO BE SO HURT AND CONFUSED BY SOMEONE LOVING ME WITH CONDITIONS,
GIVING ME A TEMPORARY LOVE THAT MAY NOT EVER LAST,

WHEN YOU HAD YEARS TO FIGURE IT OUT.

I WAS MISSING THE CONSTANT AFFECTION,
AFFECTION I ONCE OVERLOOKED DUE TO MY VISION BEING BLURRY—
BLURRY FROM THE HURT AND THE PAIN YOU CAUSED ME OVER THE YEARS.
NOW I SEE I MIGHT BE THE PROBLEM.

THESE UNKNOWN FEELINGS CAUSING HURTFUL ACTIONS,
TO INTENTIONALLY MAKE YOU FEEL WHAT I FEEL, TIMES TWO.
SUDDENLY, I'M THE HYPOCRITE,
PREACHING YOU WOULDN'T HURT THE PEOPLE YOU LOVE,
YET I HURT YOU.
BUT WAIT, I'M HURT TOO.

I HAVE TO BE A DUMMY TO BE WITH YOU,
FILL MY BRAIN WITH MESH
SO I DONT SEE THE MESS YOU CAUSE,
THE RUCKUS YOU CREATE WITH YOUR WORDS.
A CONSTANT REPLAY, BREAKING MY HEART,
TEARING ME APART,
LEAVING ME TO THINK,
"THAT'S HOW YOU TRULY FEEL ABOUT ME."
FORGETTING THE " I LOVE YOU"S AND THE "YOU'RE SO BEAUTIFUL"S,
SLITHERING BEHIND THE HURT,

TO GIVE ME A MAKEOVER OF MY BROKEN HEART—
SOMETHING I THOUGHT YOU COULD FIX,
BUT I WOULD'VE NEVER GUESSED THE FIX WAS THIS.

SHAPE-SHIFTING INTO THE SAME PEOPLE YOU WANTED
TO CAUSE PAIN TOO FOR HURTING ME,
BUT HERE I AM, HURT BY ALL THREE.

OVER IT AGAIN.
I'M SIMPLY OVER YOU AGAIN.
I'M OVER THE FEELING OF YOU.
I'M OVER EVERYTHING ABOUT YOU.
I'M OVER THE WAY YOU TALK TO ME.
I'M OVER THE WAY I CONSTANTLY TRY TO BE WITH YOU.
I'M OVER THE WAY YOU ACT LIKE I'M NOT A PERSON.
I'M OVER PUTTING MYSELF SECOND TO ACCOMMODATE YOU.
I'M OVER CONSTANTLY CONSIDERING YOU.
I'M JUST OVER YOU.

YOU DON'T BRING ME THAT GOOD FEELING ANYMORE.
I'M YOUR SECOND OPTION,
THE OPTION THAT WILL ALWAYS BE THERE.

BUT I'M NOT ANYMORE.
I DON'T NEED TO BE THERE.
SOMETHING THAT WAS ONCE SO PURE AND FULL OF LOVE—
SOMETHING I ONCE PRAYED AND CRIED ABOUT—
THAT HAS TURNED INTO SOMETHING SO PAINFUL AND REGRETFUL,
SOMETHING I WISHED I WOULD'VE LEFT THE FIRST TIME,
WISHING I HAD THE COURAGE TO NOT TURN BACK AROUND.

I'M SO PISSED RIGHT NOW.
I'M PISSED THAT WE'RE DONE.
I'M PISSED THAT I BELIEVED YOU.
IM PISSED THAT I GAVE YOU SO MUCH OF ME.
I'M PISSED THAT I GAVE YOU MORE THAN I COULD GIVE MYSELF.
I'M PISSED THAT I LOVED YOU SO MUCH.
I'M PISSED THAT I COULDN'T SEE THE MESS BEFORE IT HIT ME.
I'M PISSED THAT I LET MY GUARD DOWN WITH YOU.
I'M PISSED FOR SO MANY REASONS.
BUT MAINLY, I'M PISSED BECAUSE I TRUSTED YOU.

I DIDN'T REALIZE HOW MUCH YOU CARESSING MY BODY DID TO ME—
NOTHING SEXUALLY, OBVIOUSLY,
WELL, FOR THE TIME BEING.
YOUR ARMS AROUND MY WAIST, PULLING ME CLOSER WITH NO
SPACE IN BETWEEN US.
MY BODY TINGLING, SLOWLY HEATING UP, IM STARTING TO FEEL THE
PRESSURE BUILD UP,
BUT I EMBRACE IT—
A FEELING I MISSED FOR SO LONG,
A FEELING THAT DOES SO MUCH TO ME,
ALTERING MY BODY CHEMISTRY, PUTTING ME RIGHT TO SLEEP,
MAKING MY HEART RACE,
ON THE LOOKOUT JUST FOR YOU.

I KNOW THIS IS A ONE-TIME THING,
I ONLY WANT IT TO BE AN "OUR" THING.
THE FEELING OF YOUR HANDS RUBBING ON ME,
GIVING ME THE CHILLS ,
MAKING ME SINK DEEPER INTO YOU.

BUT RIGHT NOW, YOU'RE THE ANGEL AND I'M THE VILLAIN.
IT'S MY TURN TO RETURN THE FAVOR OF A FEELING—
OF FEELING GOOD IN MORE THAN ONE WAY,
TO SHOW YOU HOW I'M FEELING.
BUT RIGHT NOW, I UNDERSTAND WE'RE KEEPING IT PG -13.

THE BIGGEST QUESTION OF THEM ALL IS: WHY?
I ASK MYSELF WHY ALL THE TIME—
WHY THIS, WHY THAT?
WHY CAN'T YOU LET THEM GO?
WHY DO YOU NEED THEM?
WHY DID THEY DO THAT TO ME?
FOLLOWING BEHIND—
WHY ARE YOU BEING NICE?
WHAT'S YOUR AGENDA?
LIKE I DON'T DESERVE KINDNESS.

QUESTIONING YOUR INTENTIONS,
TO PREVENT BEING HURT AGAIN.

I BELIEVE YOU DID LOVE ME,
BUT YOUR LOVE HURT.
YOUR WORDS HURT.
YOUR BEHAVIORS HURT.
BLAMING ME FOR YOUR ACTIONS—
I'LL NEVER UNDERSTAND HOW THAT WORKS.

SAME LESSON, DIFFERENT PERSON.
TEACHING SOMEONE EVERYTHING ABOUT YOU,
OPENING YOURSELF UP,
BECOMING VULNERABLE.
EVERY SECRET YOU'VE SPILLED WAS A KNIFE IN YOUR BACK,
WAITING TO BE DRAGGED DOWN,
LEAVING YOU OPEN AND VULNERABLE
TO BE HURT.
ALL YOU WANTED WAS A FAIRYTALE ENDING,
BUT INSTEAD, YOU GOT YOUR VILLAIN ORIGIN STORY.

STOP AND BREATH.
YOU'RE MOVING TOO FAST.
TAKE A BREATH—
INHALE AND EXHALE.
LET ALL THE TENSION GO AWAY,
FAR AWAY,
SO FAR YOU CAN BREATHE AGAIN.
RELAX AND CLOSE YOUR EYES.
WHEN YOU WAKE UP AGAIN,
SLOW DOWN AND BREATH.
YOU'LL BE OKAY.

LOSING YOU MEANT FINDING ME.

PRAYER

EVERY TIME I PRAYED FOR ME AND YOU,
FOR US TO BE COVERED AND PROTECTED,
TO FOLLOW THE PATH MADE FOR US,
I WAS PRAYING A DIFFERENT PRAYER—
A PRAYER THAT WE WOULD SOON KNOW,
TO BRING US BACK TO EACH OTHER.

AUTOPILOT IS A STATE OF BEING WHERE YOUR BODY JUST MOVES
WITHOUT A THOUGHT,
WHERE YOUR MIND AND BODY AREN'T CONNECTING.
NOW YOU FEEL YOURSELF LAGGING,
HAVING DELAYED REACTIONS—
A FEELING OF JUST BEING HERE.

I'M IN AUTO PILOT.
I DON''T KNOW WHAT'S GOING ON, BUT IM JUST HERE, LIVING,
DOING THE SAME THING OVER AND OVER AGAIN,
FORGETTING THINGS BECAUSE THEY'RE NOT REACHING MY BRAIN,
BUT MY BODY AUTOMATICALLY DOING IT.
SO WHILE I'M LOOKING FOR MY KEYS IN PANIC,
MY BODY ALREADY GRABBED THEM AND PUT THEM IN MY JACKET.

AUTOPILOT AND AUTOMATIC ARE TWO WORDS THAT FALL TOGETHER,
BECAUSE I'M AUTOMATICALLY PUT IN AUTO PILOT
WHEN MY BRAIN AND BODY ARE WORKING AGAINST EACH OTHER,
LEAVING MY SOUL SAYING, *"SORRY."*
I NEED US ALL TO BE CONNECTED, BUT WE'RE BEING HURT.

I GUESS IT'S TRUE THAT YOUR BODY REACTS FIRST,
UNTIL IT REACHES THE SIGNALS IN YOUR BRAIN.

I HATE AUTOPILOT ME.
SHE'S SO BLAND—NO EMOTION, NO ENERGY.
SHE CAN'T CARE, BECAUSE SHE'S JUST HERE.

SHE WISHES SHE WASN'T ALWAYS IN AUTOPILOT,
BUT IT'S JUST BECOME HER SECOND NATURE.
SHE USED TO LIKE IT,
BECAUSE IT HELPED HER DISCONNECT FROM EVERYBODY,
BUT NOW SHE'S DISCONNECTING FROM HERSELF.

SHE'S HERE, BUT A DIFFERENT *HERE.*
HER BODY IS HERE,
BUT HER MIND IS SOMEWHERE ELSE.
AUTOPILOT—
A STATE OF JUST BEING HERE…

IT'S BACK,
CONFIRMING EVERYTHING THAT I LACK,
EMOTIONALLY AND MENTALLY GOING BACK
TO A PLACE I WAS DOING A FULL MARATHON TO ESCAPE—
TO NOT FEEL THIS WAY AGAIN.

TO STOP CRYING ON THE INSIDE
WHILE PRETENDING TO BE HAPPY ON THE OUTSIDE.
I'M STARTING TO WEAR THIS MASK TO WELL;
IT ALMOST FOOLED ME.

I KNEW YOU WERE COMING BACK.
I FELT MYSELF SLOWING DOWN,
BUT IT'S BECAUSE I WAS DROWNING—
DROWNING IN EMOTIONS THAT CAME FROM NOWHERE,
FORCING THIS MASK OFF FOR SOMEONE TO FINALLY SEE THE REAL ME,
THE AUTOPILOT ME.

HE NOTICES IT.
SOMEBODY FINALLY NOTICES IT.

COULD THIS BE THE MOMENT I GET BACK UP ON MY FEET
AND FINISH THE RACE?
IS THIS THE PERSON THAT CAN FIX THE BROKEN ME?

HOW CAN HE SEE ME?
IS MY MASK SO DAMAGED NOW EVERYONE CAN SEE?
I'VE BEEN IN HIDING .
WHAT ARE THEY GOING TO THINK?
"SHE'S AS SAD AS SHE LOOKS."
WILL I BECOME THE NEW TALK OF THE TOWN.
"SHE HAS GONE CRAZY."

CONTINUED.

I'M SPIRALING—
JUST DRAWING SCRIBBLES WITHOUT LIFTING ONE HAND.
WHEN WILL I BE ABLE TO DRAW A LONG, STRAIGHT LINE?
MOST IMPORTANTLY, WHEN WILL I CROSS THIS FINISH LINE?

I KNOW YOU'RE BACK,
BUT YOU'RE HERE DIFFERENTLY.
YOU'RE MORE CALM, MORE SNEAKY,
INSTEAD OF HAMMERING YOUR WAY INTO MY LIFE.

WHY ARE YOU DIFFERENT?
AM I TOO PATHETIC TO HANDLE YOU AGAIN?
DO YOU SEE HOW MUCH FIGHT I HAVE LEFT IN ME?
IT FEELS LIKE IT'S LITTLE TO NONE, IF YOU ASK ME.

BUT SINCE WE'RE ASKING QUESTIONS—
WHY ARE YOU HERE, EXACTLY?

I'M HURTING AT THE POSSIBILITY—
IT'S REALLY NO MORE *US*.

YOU HAD MY HEART IN YOUR HAND AND DROPPED IT,
SPIT ON IT, AND STOMPED ON IT.
I CAN'T EVEN BELIEVE I LET YOU HAVE ALL THIS OVER ME
I CAN'T BELIEVE I WAS DEFENDING MYSELF FROM SOMEONE I LOVED,
WOULD'VE DONE ANYTHING FOR—
SOMEONE THAT WAS SUPPOSED TO RIDE FOR ME.
BUT IT SEEMS OUR RIDE HAS STOPPED,
BECAUSE THERE'S NO MORE *US*.
THE *HONEYS* ARE GONE.
THE SWEETNESS HAS LEFT.
THERE'S NO MORE STICKINESS TO KEEP US TOGETHER.

YOU DIDN'T STITCH MY HEART—
I DID.
YOU WEREN'T THERE FOR ME LIKE YOU SAID,
WHEN I NEEDED YOU THE MOST.
BUT THE ONLY REASON I'M HURT TO THE POINT I CAN'T MANAGE
IS BECAUSE OF YOU.

SLEEP IS SOMETHING I CAN'T GET.
YOU'RE MY NEWEST NIGHTMARE,
MY NEW HORRIFYING TRUTH
YOU'RE MAKING ME LOSE SLEEP BECAUSE YOU'RE THERE.
EVERY TIME I CLOSE MY EYES, I SEE YOU WANTING OTHER GIRLS,
AND YOUR FAMILY AGREES—
A FAMILY THAT I THOUGHT I COULD CALL MINES.

IM TIRED
I JUST WANT SOME SLEEP.
BUT YOU'VE TURNED SOMETHING THAT USED TO BE SO PEACEFUL
TO SOMETHING THAT I DON'T WANT TO NEED.

DEPRESSION—
SOMETHING SO HATED,
IT SWARMS MY COMMUNITY,
ALMOST LIKE GUN VIOLENCE OR POLICE KILLINGS,
BUT THIS IS A SILENT KILLER,
A SERIAL KILLER.

ITS LIKE THE TERM PEOPLE SAY,
"I DIDN'T MAKE YOU PUT A GUN TO YOUR HEAD,"
BUT YET YOU DID.
YOU'VE TAKEN SO MANY LIVES BY THE GUN TO THE HEAD,
MEDS IN THE BED,
STRESS IN THE HEAD.

YOU LEAVE SO MANY BROKEN HEARTS WHEN YOU COME AROUND,
FROM THE PEOPLE YOU TOUCH TO THEIR LOVED ONES THAT CAN'T TOUCH THEM ANYMORE.
A DISEASE SO STRONG THAT IT'S INVINCIBLE.
SHOOT, IT'S INVISIBLE TO THOSE THAT DON'T HAVE IT,
BUT TO THOSE THAT DO, IT'S A HUGE THUNDERSTORM
THAT RAINS ON THE HAPPY DAYS—
DAYS WE'VE TAKEN FOR GRANTED,
BUT LEARNED TO BE SO MUCH MORE APPRECIATIVE OF AFTER EACH STORM.

A STORM THAT PEOPLE BELIEVE WE SHOULDN'T HAVE.
"YOU HAVE NOTHING TO BE DEPRESSED ABOUT."
WHY, THANK YOU, GENIUS, FOR TELLING ME SOMETHING I ALREADY KNOW.
WITH THAT SINGLE PHRASE, YOU RAISED IT UP OUT OF ME,
TO PROVE TO ME AGAIN THAT I'M LIKE THIS FOR NO REASON,
LEAVING ANOTHER MARK, A MARK I HAD TO FIGHT HARD TO COVER UP—
A BATTLE SCAR ONLY I WILL KNOW OF.
A BATTLE I FOUGHT ALONE,
A BATTLE I HAD TO HEAL FROM—
THE SCARIEST BATTLE I'VE EVER HAD TO FIGHT.
BUT TO YOU,
IM JUST AN UNGRATEFUL, RUDE , SELFISH, ANGRY CHILD
BUT, MOM,
IT'S JUST DEPRESSION—
SOMETHING YOU'VE MIGHT'VE CAUSED.

THEY SAY WHEN YOU FIND A GOOD A PERSON, THAN CHERISH THEM.
SO, AM I NOT A GOOD PERSON?
AM I NOTHING WORTH CHERISHING?
AM I ONLY WORTH THE TEMPORARY EMOTIONS AND EXCITEMENT ?

QUESTIONS NOBODY SHOULD EVER HAVE TO ASK,
THINGS I WOULDN'T EVEN WISH ON THE DEVIL HIMSELF...

I WANTED YOU, I FOUGHT FOR YOU, I LOVED YOU.
I NOTICED WHEN I TALKED ABOUT YOU,
I WAS TALKING TO THE PAST—
BEFORE ALL THIS HAPPENED.
BEFORE I FELT ALL OF THIS .

YOU MAY HAVE WANTED ME AND LOVED ME,
BUT FOUGHT FOR US?
NEVER.
IT ALWAYS HAD TO BE EQUAL,
OR I HAD TO GO ABOVE ,
FOR SOMETHING THAT WAS IN THE PAST.

I JUST WANTED YOU TO CHOOSE ME THE WAY I DO,
BUT THAT'S THE PROBLEM—YOU DID.
YOU CHOSE EVERYONE ELSE BUT ME.
THAT'S WHY IT HURTS.

I WAS COMPLETELY WILLING TO BE SINGLE AND IN A RELATIONSHIP JUST FOR YOU,
BUT YOU KNEW ME TO WELL.
YOU KNOW *YOU* TO WELL.

AND I KNOW THIS IS GOING TO HURT ME LIKE HELL,
BUT THESE ARE JUST THE CARDS THAT I WAS DEALT.
NOTHING ABOUT THIS IS GOING TO BE PAINLESS, AND I KNOW THIS.
BUT BOY, DID I WISH I DIDN'T HAVE TO FEEL THIS.

THIS FEELING, SO HURTFUL THAT IT JUST MAKES ME WEEP,
 CRYING AT RANDOM MOMENTS BECAUSE MOMENTS LIKE SUCH CUTS SO DEEP,
AND MAKE A MARK OF NO RETURN.
WHEN ALL I WISH FOR IS ANOTHER TURN—
TO TURN BACK TIME FOR YOU TO CHOOSE US, FOR YOU TO CHOOSE ME,
AND TOGETHER WE'D RULE THE WORLD THAT TRIED TO DESTROY US,
AND PROVE THE PEOPLE AROUND US
THEY DON'T KNOW US.
BUT MOST IMPORTANTLY, I'LL FINALLY CHOOSE ME.

I'M FEELING STAGNANT,
COMPLACENT.
LIFE IS MOVING ALONG, BUT IM LIVING THE SAME LIFE EVERYDAY
NOTHING HAS CHANGED.
MY OLD HABITS ARE SNEAKING BACK IN,
DROWNING OUT MY NEW WAYS—
QUICKER THAN ME STEPPING IN QUICKSAND.
IT'S JUST BEEN TO MUCH.

IM GOING BACK INTO HIDING,
BUT WHAT AM I HIDING FROM?
THE WORLD?
PUSHING EVERYTHING TO THE SIDE AND MOVING ON LIKE MY LIFE IS
NOT BEING AFFECTED BY THIS.
I'M SCREAMING FROM THE INSIDE, BUT NOBODY NOTICES.
HONESTLY, I STOPPED NOTICING IT.

I JUST NEED TO GET AWAY FROM EVERYBODY, INCLUDING MYSELF.
BUT HOW CAN I LEAVE ME?
I CAN CHANGE MY APPEARANCE, BUT THAT'S NOT CHANGING ME—
IT'S JUST CHANGING HOW I LOOK.
I WANT TO LEAVE THIS OLD ME AND STEP INTO THIS NEW ME,
BUT I GUESS THIS IS GOD SHOWING ME YOU HAVE TO LET GO OF THE
OLD THINGS AND OLD WAYS
TO LET THE NEW AND IMPROVED WAYS IN.
BUT HOW DO I JUST LEAVE ME?
HOW DO I LEAVE SOMETHING I'VE KNOWN FOR SO LONG?

I'M JUST TIRED OF FEELING STUCK.

YOU SAY IT'S IRRELEVANT TO ME, BUT IT'S NOT.
IT'S WEIGHING HEAVY ON MY HEART
AND RUNNING SPRINTS IN MY MIND
BUT BECAUSE YOU DON'T WANT TO TALK ABOUT IT,
IT'S IRRELEVANT.
BUT IT'S NOT.
ITS VERY MUCH RELEVANT,
BUT YOU DON'T WANT TO FACE THE TRUTH.
BUT IT DOESN'T MATTER,
BECAUSE ALL OF THIS IS CAUSED OVER SOMETHING
THAT'S "IRRELEVANT."

I'M NO LONGER A LOVER GIRL.
I WAS A GIRL THAT DIDN'T RECEIVE LOVE,
ONLY HURT.
IT COULDN'T BE THAT HARD TO LOVE SOMEONE LIKE ME,
BUT NOW I THINK IT'S CONTAGIOUS.
WILL THIS HURT FOLLOW ME AROUND FOREVER?
WILL I CONTINUE TO GIVE AND JUST GET HURT,
OR WILL I PUT MY FOOT DOWN AND STAND WITH RESPECT?
THE RESPECT I WISH PEOPLE WOULD GIVE ME.

TEARS FULL TO THE RIM WITH ONE BLINK.
THE WATERFALL STARTS—
A WATERFALL NO LONGER BEAUTIFUL, BUT A SAD WATERFALL.
A CURRENT SO STRONG IT SWEEPS ME UNDER,
THROWING ME ALL OVER THE PLACE,
UNTIL I FIND THE BEAUTY WITHIN THE PAIN.

I'VE BECOME FULL WITH EMOTIONS,
ATTEMPTING TO LIE ABOUT MY TRUE FEELINGS.
LYING ABOUT WANTING TO CRY,
LYING ABOUT YOU STILL AFFECTING ME,
SO I CAN DENY NOT BEING OKAY.
I KNOW IN DUE TIME I'LL BE FINE —
ACTUALLY, I'LL BE OKAY,
OKAY WITH YOU BEING A MEMORY,
NO LONGER HAUNTING ME.
YOU'VE BECOME A GHOST OF MY PAST.

I'M NO LONGER
ABLE TO BE THIS GIRL THAT YOU WANT.
I'M NOT THE GIRL THAT WANTS TO BE HIDDEN,
I'M NOT THE GIRL THAT DOESN'T WANT TO BE AMBITIOUS.
I DON'T WANT TO BE THE GIRL THAT'S BEEN AMBUSHED
BY YOUR IMPULSIVE THOUGHTS.
I'VE HAD PEACE WITHOUT YOU,
I JUST WISH WE COULD GO BACK TO WHEN IT WAS PEACE WITH YOU.
NOW IT'S NO LONGER THAT—
JUST BICKERING,
AND EVERY WORD THAT COMES OUT OF YOUR MOUTH
FLICKERS MY WANT AND DESIRE FOR YOU.
IT WAS STARTING TO FADE, LIKE A THUNDERSTORM,
HAVING NO MORE EMOTION,
GOING BACK TO THE SUNNY BLUE SKY
WE WISH TO LAY BACK AND SEE.

I STATE MY CASE
IN FRONT OF THE JURY OF MY LIFE.
GOD AS MY JUDGE,
I PEACEFULLY PLEAD GUILTY—
GUILTY OF ANY PAIN THAT I'VE CAUSED
GUILTY FOR THE PAIN THAT YOU'VE CAUSED ME.
I TOOK IT TO HIM, FOR HIM TO SENTENCE ME,
TO GUIDE ME IN THIS THING WE CALL LIFE.

SOMETHING I WISH WAS HAPPY AND RAINBOWS,
BUT EVEN THE BEST OF THE BEST GETS DESTROYED.

HERE I AM, FIGHTING TO HOLD ON A LITTLE LONGER.
I'M TOO BLIND TO SEE WHAT EVERYONE WARNED ME OF,
TELLING ME TO PULL AWAY BEFORE HE LEADS YOU ASTRAY.
BUT ALL I CAN THINK ABOUT IS THE LOVE OF MY LIFE.

THE TIGHT HOLD WE ONCE HAD
HAS NOW BECOME LOOSE.
I WISH I COULD GET OVER THIS COLD OF BEING IN LOVE.

YOU'RE FINALLY GETTING YOUR ONLY WISH,
AND THAT'S NOT TO BE WITH ME.
YOU'VE FINALLY LOST ME.

A LONG FAREWELL

FAREWELL TO ALL THE PAIN IVE BEEN THROUGH IN THIS ROOM,
FOUR WALLS THAT HAVE EXPERIENCED ALL MY SEASONS,
THAT HAVE MET NEW PEOPLE WITH ME.
A NON-JUDGEMENT ZONE FULL OF EMOTION.
I HAVE TO FINALLY SAY FAREWELL TO MY OWN SPACE,
MY SAFE SPACE, MY SAFE HAVEN.
BUT WHEN I FIRST MOVED, IT FELT LIKE HEAVEN—
LIVING IN A UNFAMILIAR AREA,
NEW RULES,
NEW PEOPLE ,
NEW LIFE .
BUT I WAS ABLE TO HAVE MY OWN LIFE.
EVEN THOUGH FRESHMAN YEAR CAME TO AN END,
I'VE SAID FAREWELL TO SO MUCH THROUGHOUT MY TIME HERE.
GOODBYE TO MY FIRST LOVER,
THE BOY I THOUGHT I WOULD BE WITH FOREVER,
THE FIRST BOY I ALLOWED TO SEE ME VULNERABLE AND CRY,
THE BOY THAT SHATTERED MY HEART INTO A MILLION PIECES.
THESE FOUR WALLS SAW EVERY INTERACTION AND EVEN ENDURED
ABUSE IN THE PROCESS.
I COULD CONFESS EVERYTHING I NEEDED TO BECAUSE NO ONE ELSE
WOULD GET IT OUT OF **THESE FOUR WALLS.**
THEY SAW ME GROW INTO A BETTER VERSION OF MYSELF—
SETTING BOUNDARIES,
LETTING GO OF PEOPLE WHO I THOUGHT LOVED ME,
WORKING ON MY TEMPER,
AND JUST FINDING ME.
FAREWELL TO MY ROOMMATES,
THE PEOPLE WHO KEPT ME TOGETHER,
THE ONES WHO BECAME MY ELMERS TO MY GLUE.
WE BONDED TOGETHER AND HOPEFULLY CREATED A FOREVER
CONNECTION.
IT WAS TRULY A BLESSING TO HAVE Y'ALL NEXT TO ME.
THANK YOU FOR PUSHING ME TO EXPERIENCE A DIFFERENT ME.

YOU WON
I'VE ALWAYS BEEN PLAYING A ONE-SIDED GAME—
A GAME WHERE I JUST FIGHT FOR YOUR LOVE,
BUT MY LOVE IS SO EASY TO LET GO.
THE MORE I FIGHT, THE MORE WORTHLESS I FEEL, SO I STOP.
THEN YOU TRY, I TRY, AND YOU STOP.
IT'S A VICIOUS GAME OF BACK AND FORTH,
UNTIL YOU DECIDE WHAT YOU WANT,
AND IT'S NOT ME.

I DON'T KNOW WHY.
I DON'T KNOW WHY I TRY TO TALK TO A BRICK WALL,
HOPING THAT IT WILL TUMBLE AND FALL AFTER HEARING MY ROARING EMOTIONS.
MY WORDS MOVE LIKE A BULLDOZER, AND AFTER EVERY WORD,
I ATTACK IN HOPES TO SEE WHAT'S BEHIND THE WALL.
BUT BEHIND IT IS A BROKEN PERSON WAITING TO BE HEALED,
WHILE LOOKING FOR A REASON TO STAY HURT .

SO YOU DECIDE TO COUNTERACT ME AND BREAK MY WALL DOWN,
TO HURT THE GIRL WITH PURE LOVE,
TO TURN IT INTO YOUR LOVE,
BECAUSE YOU KNOW HOW TO MANEUVER
HOW TO MANIPULATE,
TO BECOME THE VICTIM.
A HEART BROKEN BOY BREAKING A GIRL'S HEART,
WITH EACH SWIFT MOTION AND WORD.

SHE BUILDS HER WALL UP,
HOPING YOU WOULD RETREAT BACK TO WHERE YOU CAME FROM.
BUT NOW YOU'RE ON A HUNT FOR HER LOVE—
A LOVE LIKE NO OTHER,
A RARE LOVE,
A NURTURING LOVE,
A LOVE YOU TOOK FOR GRANTED, USED, AND ABUSED.
A LOVE EVERY MAN IS FEENING FOR,
BUT WHY TRY WHEN I GAVE MY ALL TO YOU?
THAT'S ALL I WANTED TO DO;
GIVE YOU ALL MY LOVE.

BUT NOW I'M HALF-LOVING PEOPLE, THINKING THAT IT'S HELPING ME.
IN REALITY, IT'S TURNING ME INTO A COLD MONSTER THAT I DON'T WANT TO BE.
IT'S TURNING ME INTO YOU—
BUT A DIFFERENT VERSION OF YOU.
IT'S ME AND YOU MIXED,
AND I'M STILL TRYING TO FIND THE "ME" IN ALL OF IT.

YOU'VE CREPT BEHIND MY WALL TO SPY ON ME,
TO SEE MY DEFENSE SYSTEM,
NOTICING MY IMPERFECTIONS AND WHERE YOU CAN DO THE MOST DAMAGE.
AFTER TAKING MONTHS OF ANALYZING,
YOU FINALLY PUT YOUR PLAN IN MOTION.
NOW YOU'RE RUNNING FULL FORCE AT ME,
TRYING TO BREAK THE WALL I PUT IN DEFENSE FROM YOU.
STILL SEEING IF YOUR SPECIALS MOVES WILL CAUSE DAMAGE,
AND HAVE THE SAME EFFECT ON ME.

BUT AS ALWAYS, THEY DO.
NOW I CAN HOLD A POKER FACE,
BECAUSE I'VE BECOME YOU—
I KNOW YOUR GAME:
THE GAME OF LOVE AND HATE,
THE GAME TO MANIPULATE.
BUT ALL IT DOES IS REMIND ME WHY THE WALL WAS BUILT IN THE FIRST PLACE—
BECAUSE OF YOU.
SO, EVERY TIME YOU HURT ME, IT HURTS LESS.
BUT I DON'T KNOW WHY I WOULD LET MY GUARD DOWN FOR YOU EVER AGAIN.

TO MY LAST LOVER,
THANK YOU FOR EVERYTHING YOU'VE TAUGHT ME.
IT WASN'T MUCH ABOUT LIFE,
BUT IT WAS MUCH ABOUT ME—
HOW I WANT TO BE TREATED,
HOW I *DIDN'T* WANT TO BE TREATED,
HOW I WANT TO BE HELD,
AND WHAT I NEEDED TO WORK ON.

TO MY LAST LOVER
ALL I WANTED WAS SUPPORT—
SOMETHING YOU COULD NEVER GIVE ME.
I DIDN'T REALIZE HOW MUCH SUPPORT COULD DO FOR A PERSON.
IT WAS THE ICING ON THE CAKE FOR YOU TO ALWAYS BE THERE FOR ME;
TO CATER TO EMOTIONS,
NURTURE MY HEART,
A SPECIAL KISS TO MY FOREHEAD.
NOW, IT COULDN'T BE NOTHING.

INSTEAD, YOU MADE ME FEEL LIKE I'M WHERE I'M AT TODAY BECAUSE OF YOU,
YET ALL YOU SEEMED TO DO WAS DESTROY ME.
YOU THOUGHT YOU COVERED THE WHOLE BOARD,
BUT YOU BARELY COVERED A QUARTER.
NOW I HAVE TO MAKE SURE I'M COVERED
AND PROTECTED—FROM YOU.

SO YOUR WORDS WON'T BE A PUNCH TO THE FACE ANYMORE.
THEY'VE BECOME A PAPER CUT—
SOMETHING YOU DON'T SEE OR FEEL UNTIL YOU PUT SOMETHING ON IT.

I KNOW HOW IT FEELS TO BE NURTURED AND CARED FOR—
TO BE TREATED GENTLY.
NOT WANTING TO OVERSTEP,
BUT BEING CAREFUL WITH ME.
TO KNOW WHEN I SAY I'M PRECIOUS CARGO,
YOU WOULD *SEE* THAT I'M THE DIAMOND YOU HAVE TO KEEP SAFE—
TO PROTECT WITH ALL YOUR MIGHT.
TO BE TOUGH ON THE OUTSIDE TO KEEP ME SAFE,
AND PRESERVE MY VALUE.

JUST WHY?
I'M TIRED OF ASKING MYSELF THIS QUESTION.
WHY AM I HURT BY YOU?
WHY DO I ALLOW YOU TO AFFECT ME?
WHY CAN'T I HATE YOU ?
WHY AM I STILL IN LOVE WITH YOU?
WHY DO I WANT TO BE UP UNDER YOU?
WHY CAN'T I JUST HURT YOU HOW I'M HURTING?
WHY AM I STILL FIGHTING?

JUST WHY.

OUR RITUAL
THE BEGINNING OF EVERY MONTH,
YOU CHOOSE TO LEAVE WHEN I CHOOSE TO STAY.
BY NOW, I SHOULD KNOW MY PLACE—
IT DOESN'T SEEM TO BE WITH YOU ANYMORE.

EVERYTIME YOU LEAVE, YOU HURT ME
IN WAYS THAT YOU PROMISED YOU WOULDN'T DARE.
HERE I AM, WISHING THINGS WERE DIFFERENT,
TRYING TO PUT TOGETHER THE MISSING PIECES
OF SOMETHING I DIDN'T BREAK IN THE FIRST PLACE,
WHILE YOU PUT THE BLAME ON ME,
MAKING ME QUESTION MY WORTH.

BUT I KNOW YOU'LL MAKE ME HIGH
OFF YOUR TEMPORARY LOVE,
UNTIL I FORGET ABOUT OUR RITUAL—
JUST FOR YOU TO REMIND ME NEXT MONTH
NEVER GET TO COMFORTABLE.

MY THOUGHTS ARE CHANGING,
FEELINGS ARE CHANGING TOO.
I DON'T KNOW WHAT TO DO.
I CAN'T HANDLE NOT HAVING YOU,
BUT I CAN'T HANDLE HAVING YOU TOO.

WE'RE PLAYING AT OUR HEARTS LIKE A VIOLIN,
RIPPING EVERY STRING AFTER EVERY STROKE.
I REALLY DO JUST WANT TO BE LOVED BY YOU,
HELD BY YOU,
KISSED BY YOU.
BUT NOW, I'M NOT.
I COULDN'T EVEN CHERISH THE LAST MEMORY WITH YOU.
I GUESS THAT'S WHY THEY SAY,
"CHERISH EVERY MOMENT,
BECAUSE YOU DON'T KNOW WHEN WILL BE YOU LAST."

I'M SCARED OF CREATING A LOVE SO DEEP
THAT I FORGET HOW BAD LOVE REALLY IS.
BUT IS LOVE REALLY THAT BAD?

I TEND TO FIND MYSELF HERE A LOT—
ALONE,
BY MYSELF.

THEY SHOULD BE ABLE TO SEE ME,
AT LEAST LIKE I WANT THEM TO.
I JUST NEEDED TO BE HELD,
BUT I GOT HURT.
I JUST WANT TO CRY,
BUT I DON'T KNOW WHAT ABOUT.

THIS IS SO STUPID.
I JUST WANT TO BE ALONE—
ALONE FOREVER,
WITH NOBODY HERE
AND NOBODY THERE—
JUST ME,
MYSELF,
AND I.

NEVER ALONE
I DON'T WANT TO BE ALONE—
AND I KNOW THIS.
I WANT TO BE HAPPY,
LIVING A PEACEFUL LIFE WITH SOMEONE THAT MAKES ME HAPPY,
SOMEONE WHO CATERS TO ME.
I DON'T WANT THIS LIFE—
THIS LIFE OF SOMEONE PICKING ME
WHEN IT'S CONVENIENT FOR THEM.
MY HEART ACHES,
GETTING CRUSHED EVERY TIME.

THE ONE PERSON I STILL WANT TO CHOOSE ME
WON'T.
AND THAT'S WHY IT HURTS.
YOU'RE NOT THE ONE THAT NEEDS TO CHOOSE ME.

I WAS SO CAUGHT UP IN YOUR GAZE,
I LOST ADMIRATION.
THE THINGS I WOULD SOON LOVE—
YOU'VE MADE ME HATE THEM,
DEGRADING THEM TO BE NOTHING SPECIAL.

YOU WANTED ME TO CHANGE
THE VERY THING THAT SET ME APART—
MY IMPERFECTIONS.
YOU FELT LIKE YOU COULD WALK OVER ME.

BUT I TOOK YOUR ADVICE
AND STOOD UP TALL,
TALLER THEN THE DESIRES I HAD FOR YOU.

I WAS SO CAUGHT UP IN YOU,
YOU HAD TO FIND SOMETHING TO BRING ME DOWN,
TO MAKE ME BELIEVE
I WASN'T SOMETHING SPECIAL.

I'VE FINALLY FOUND MY BEAUTY—
SOMETHING THAT WAS STRIPPED
WITH THE LACK OF SECURITY.

**I'VE FINALLY FOUND MY PURPOSE,
NO LONGER HOPELESS.**

IT STARTED WITH YOU—
HOW YOU TREAT ME AND VIEW ME.
IT STARTED WITH YOU—
HOW YOU LOVED ME AND TOOK CARE OF ME.
IT STARTED WITH YOU.

NOW, EVERY OTHER GUY THAT COMES INTO MY LIFE
TREATS ME THE SAME EXACT WAY—
THE WAY I WANT TO BE TREATED BY YOU.
BUT YET, THEY'RE THE SAME AS YOU.

YOU WIN.
YOU'VE FINALLY WON THIS TRICKY GAME WE'VE BEEN PLAYING—
THE GAME OF BACK AND FORTH,
THE GAME OF WHO HURT WHO THE WORST.

I DON'T HAVE IT IN ME ANYMORE TO HURT YOU.
I DON'T HAVE IT IN ME ANYMORE TO LET YOU AFFECT ME,
TO FOCUS ON THE WRONG THINGS,
THE THINGS YOU NO LONGER SHOULD PLAY A FACTOR IN.

I STILL LOVE YOU,
BUT I'VE FINALLY FOUND THAT I LOVED MYSELF MORE—
MORE THAN I BELIEVE YOU DID.

I HAD TO FIND THE LINE BETWEEN LOVE AND LUST,
AND I KNEW WHICH ONE WAS US.
I JUST ALWAYS TRIED TO DENY IT.
I THINK THAT'S WHAT FINALLY MADE ME OVER US—
LUST.

BECAUSE I REALIZED SEX WASN'T EVERYTHING.
SO YOU NO LONGER HAD A USE FOR ME,
BECAUSE I STOPPED REQUIRING THE ONLY THING YOU REQUIRED.
BUT I GREW TIRED OF THE SAME THING OVER AND OVER AGAIN.
I NEVER GREW TIRED OF THE IDEA OF LOVE,
ESPECIALLY YOURS.

BUT I'VE LET YOU AND LUST WIN.
I HOPE IT'S EVERYTHING YOU WANTED,
BECAUSE AT THE END OF THE DAY, LOVE IS THE END GOAL.
BUT I'VE TRIED BOTH AND LOST THE GAME.
SO CONGRATULATIONS ON THIS WIN.

LADIES, STOP SERVING THAT MAN LIKE HE'S YOUR GOD.
ALLOWING HIM TO MANIPULATE YOU IN ORDER FOR YOU TO SUMBIT,
WHEN ALL HE CAN DO IS HIT—
AS IF HE DOESN'T ALREADY REAP THE BENEFITS .

WHILE HE COMMANDS YOU TO FOLLOW HIS EVERY DEMAND,
LIKE YOU'RE SUPPOSED TO GIVE A DAMN.
AS IF YOU'RE SUPPOSED TO PUT A MAN BEFORE YOURSELF,
AS IF HE'S ALL YOU HAVE TO LOOK FORWARD TO.

HONESTLY, TO THE MOTHERS—
CURSE Y'ALL FOR SHOWING YOUR DAUGHTERS
THEY SHOULDN'T LEAVE A MAN THAT DOESN'T FIND HER WORTHY ENOUGH
TO WORSHIP THE GROUND SHE WALKS ON,
AS IF SHE ISN'T WORTHY OF HIS LOVE.
ALL BECAUSE HE CLAIMS HE CAN PROVIDE,
EVEN THOUGH WE'VE SEEN WITH OUR VERY OWN EYES
THE ONLY THING HE PROVIDES IS HURT.

CURSE YALL FOR NOT TEACHING YOUR SONS
TO KEEP A GOOD A GIRL WHEN HE FINDS HER,
FOR NOT TEACHING THEM HOW TO TREASURE TRUE LOVE,
BECAUSE A PURE LOVE LIKE THAT IS A LOVE THAT THEY'LL NEVER FORGET.

I WANTED TO BE TREATED GENTLY,
BECAUSE I'VE NEVER HAD THE BABY TREATMENT—
SOMETHING EVERYONE EXPECTS ME TO HAVE SINCE I'M THE YOUNGEST. .

THAT TITLE CREATED RESENTMENT,
TOO MUCH ATTENTION AND EXPECTATIONS,
WHEN ALL I WANTED WAS TO BEEN SEEN—
PAST MY BEAUTIFUL PHYSIQUE,
TO MY BROKEN SOUL
THAT WAS CAUSED BY BEING THE BABY.

NOW THAT I'M GROWN, I CAN'T BE A BABY .
I HAVE TO BE A TODDLER,
WANTING TO BE TREATED LIKE A BABY,
WHILE PROVING I'M A BIG GIRL AND CAN DO IT BY MYSELF.
LITTLE DO Y'ALL KNOW,
THIS LITTLE GIRL NEEDS HELP.

EVERY "NO"
EVERY HIT,
EVERY INAPPROPRIATE TOUCH
CAME CRASHING ONTO HER LIKE SHE WAS GETTING STONED.

BECOMING THE NEWEST FOUND STATUE,
CREATED BY THE MEN IN HER LIFE,
BECOMING BITS AND PIECES OF THEIR BLOOD, SWEAT, AND TEARS—
THEIR BATTLES AND THEIR VICTORIES.

NOW, I CAN'T GET A VICTORY,
BECASUE THE BATTLE IS STILL IN ME.
I NO LONGER WANT TO BE THIS WAY;
I WANT SOMEONE TO SEE ME AS ME,
NOT JUST THIS PRETTY LITTLE THING,
BUT TO SEE WHAT MADE ME—
WITHOUT HAVING TO BREAK ME TO DO SO.
TO STARE INTO MY EYES TO SEE
THAT IT'S A PERSON TRAPPED INSIDE,
BECOMING IT'S PRISONER OF LIFE.

I'VE BECOME A PRODUCT OF DESTRUCTION.

A GIRL THAT NO LONGER EXIST
THE SOUND OF HER NAME FADES AWAY.
WITH EACH DAY, SHE BECOMES A LITTLE LESS OF HERSELF.
THE SMILE THAT ONCE BRIGHTENED UP THE NEXT PERSON DAY
HAS NOW BEEN WIPED AWAY,
TRAPPED IN A BOX THAT CANNOT BE OPENED.
A LAUGH THAT FILLED THE ROOM IN A JOYFUL HARMONY
IS NOW MUTED.

A GIRL THAT HAS FADED AWAY.

SILENCE IS GOOD.
SILENCE SHOWED ME HOW DEEPLY I FEEL,
HOW MUCH I CARE,
WHY THINGS HURT SO MUCH.
BUT IT MAKES ME CURIOUS—
MAKES ME WONDER,
MAKES ME THINK,
FINDING COMFORT WITHIN MYSELF.

CLOUDING MY OWN VISION,
I CAN SEE ALL THE FAIRYTALES,
THE POSSIBILITIES,
THE WHAT IF'S,
THE ENDLESS STORYLINES TO OUR STORY—
THE STORY THAT ENDED IN SILENCE.

DID I LOSE YOU?
DID I LOSE THE PERSON THAT WOULD BE THERE FOR ME,
THE PERSON THAT CARED FOR ME,
THE PERSON THAT LISTENED TO ME,
THE PERSON THAT PULLED ME OUT OF DEPRESSION,
THE PERSON THAT LOVED ME FIRST,
MY FIRST LOVE?
DID I LOSE YOU?

THE PERSON I RUN TO,
THE PERSON THAT GIVE ME INTERNAL HUGS,
THE PERSON THAT FEELS EVERYTHING I FEEL,
THE PERSON GOING THROUGH THIS WITH ME,
DID I LOSE YOU?

OR DID I LOSE THE OLD VERSION OF YOU,
THE VERSION EVERYONE COULD USE AND ABUSE?

DID I LOSE YOU?
YES, YOU LOST ME...
I WONDERED WHY IT WAS SO EASY FOR HIM TO DO THIS TO ME
WITHOUT ME SEEING IT,
BUT WE BOTH BLENDED INTO EACH OTHER'S BACKGROUNDS,
WE WERE TOO DEEP IN TO REALIZE IT.
I LOST THE PERSON YOU KNEW AND FELL IN LOVE WITH...
WHO I'M BECOMING...
THE WOMAN I'M FALLING IN LOVE WITH,
THE ONE THAT DOESN'T ANSWER ANYMORE,
THE ONE THAT VOCALIZES HER FEELINGS,
THE ONE THAT DOESN'T FORCE SOMEONE TO LISTEN,
TO CARE, OR WANT HER,
THE ONE THAT SPOILS HERSELF,
THE ONE THAT CARES FOR HERSELF,
THE ONE I NEEDED YEARS AGO.
IM BECOMING THE ONE TO SHOW HER THAT I GOT US.

DID I LOSE YOU?
YES, BUT YOU ALSO FOUND ME...

**THE MEMORIES WILL CREEP UP,
MAKING YOU QUESTION IF MOVING ON IS THE BEST OPTION.**

THE GIRL THAT ONCE WANTED TO BE SEEN, FELT, AND HEARD
IS NOW GONE
SHE DISAPPEARED IN THE HOWLING WIND AS THE DARK NIGHT SWEPT US OFF OUR FEET
INTO THE HAUNTING THOUGHTS
REMINISCING OF THE GIRL THAT HAD DISAPPEARED.

I WANT SOMEONE THAT CAN LEAD,
SOMEONE I CAN LEARN FROM,
SOMEONE I CAN FOLLOW WITHOUT QUESTIONING THEIR EVERY STEP,
SOMEONE THAT IS GENTLE AND LOVING,
SOMEONE THAT MAKES ME NOT WANT TO DISAPPEAR.

WHAT AM I FIGHTING FOR?
FOR A LOVE THAT DOESN'T EXIST?
FOR A GUY SO FAR UP HIS OWN ASS HE CAN'T SEE HIS OWN SHIT?
FOR A BROKEN HEART TO BE HEALED BY AN UNHEALED PERSON?
BY THE PERSON THAT BROKE ME?
THE PERSON I LOST MYSELF FOR COUNTLESS OF TIMES,
THE PERSON I LET BREAK ME WHILE I BUILT THEM,
THE PERSON I THOUGHT I NEEDED,
THE PERSON I WANTED.
I THOUGHT I SHOULD'VE BEEN FIGHTING YOUR FIGHT WITH YOU,
BUT I DIDN'T EXPECT TO BE FIGHTING MINE ALONE.
I WANTED TO KNOW WHEN I FELT DEFEATED,
I HAD SOMEBODY TO COME HUG ME AND PICK ME BACK UP,
BUT THAT PERSON COULDN'T HAVE BEEN YOU.
SO WHAT WAS I FIGHTING FOR?
FOR ME TO BE BROKEN AND LOST?
FOR ME TO FEEL MY HEART BEING SQUEEZED SO TIGHT IN MY CHEST
THAT I COULDN'T BREATH?
FOR MY MIND BEING SO FAR GONE THAT I WAS LIVING IN A DAZE FOR MONTHS,
LIVING THE SAME DAY OVER AND OVER AGAIN?

CONTINUED.

I LET LOOSE WITH YOU.
I JUST MELTED IN YOUR ARMS EVERY TIME I FELT YOUR WARMTH.
YOU WERE HOME, MY SAFE SPACE.
THAT'S WHAT I WAS FIGHTING FOR?
FEELING SAFE SO I DIDN'T HAVE TO WORRY ABOUT ANYTHING IN THE WORLD.
YOU MADE MY WORLD STOP.
ALL THE BAD TURNED GOOD UNTIL IT STOPPED TURNING BAD .
YOU GAVE ME THE DEFINITION OF "GOOD THINGS COME TO AN END…"
SO AGAIN,
WHAT WAS I FIGHTING FOR ?

YOU'RE A BREATH OF FRESH AIR,
A NEW PAIR OF CLEAN WHITE SOCKS,
THE WIND BLOWING THROUGH MY HAIR.
YOU'RE REFRESHING, BUT NO GOOD FOR ME RIGHT NOW.
YOU'VE TAUGHT ME SO MUCH IN SO LITTLE,
BROUGHT MY EXPECTATIONS HIGH IN NO TIME.
BUT I HAVE TO LET YOU GO.
THIS FEELS LIKE MY FIRST LOVE LEAVING AGAIN.
WELL, IS IT LOVE ? IT CAN'T BE …
YOU FELT GOOD, AND I DIDN'T EVEN FEEL YOU.
YOUR WORDS FELT GOOD; THEY WERE WARM, GENTLE, AND GENUINE.
I WAS INSTANTLY COMFORTABLE WITH YOU, BUT NOW I THINK I'VE CAUGHT FEELINGS.
I WAS HOPING YOU DIDN'T KISS ME, BUT IN THE BACK OF MY HEAD,
I WANTED TO KNOW WHAT IT FELT LIKE—
IF I WOULD PULL BACK OR LEAN IN FURTHER.
SCARED TO TRY SOMETHING NEW,
MAYBE IT'LL BE REFRESHING.

CRYING IS SUCH A STRONG EMOTION.
YOU CAN FEEL THE BUILD OF TEARS, WAITING FOR THE GATES TO FINALLY OPEN,
TO FREELY FALL DOWN YOUR FACE.
IT'S AN EMOTIONAL REACTION THAT EXPRESSES MANY THINGS.
FOR ME, OFTEN IT'S SADNESS OR ANGER.
I HATE CRYING BECAUSE IT'S NOT JUST TEARS ROLLING DOWN MY FACE,
IT'S THE EMOTIONS THROUGHOUT MY BODY THAT JUST MAKES ME FEEL LIFELESS,
CLUELESS.

MOST OF THE TIME, I DON'T EVEN KNOW WHY I'M CRYING.
IT'S JUST A WAY MY BODY SHOWS ME THAT I'M TRYING,
AND THAT I FEEL SOMETHING,
EVEN IF IT'S NOT GOOD.
AT LEAST IT'S SOMETHING.

I WONDER WHY—
THIS IS WHEN I GET THE BEST SLEEP.
I ASK MYSELF ALL THE TIME,
BUT IT'S WHEN MY BODY STARTS IT'S RELEASES
ALL THE BUILT-UP HURT, ANGER, AND SADNESS.
IT ROAMS LIKE A WILD ANIMAL IN THE JUNGLE,
BUT I'M NOT HUNTING FOR ANYTHING,
THE THING THAT KEEPS TRIGGERING THE GATES.
I JUST WANT IT TO STOP WITHOUT A DEBATE.
I'M DONE FEELING LIKE A LOST PUPPY WITH MY EMOTIONS.
WHEN I FEEL THE TEARS LOADING UP,
ALL I CAN DO IS FREEZE.

WHY AM I STILL THINKING ABOUT YOU

YOU'RE ON MY MIND, JUST TAKING UP TIME—
TIME TO THINK A DIFFERENT THOUGHT,
BUT IT JUST SEEMS TO BE ALL ABOUT YOU.

I CAN FINALLY SAY I HAVE AN ADDICTION, AND IT'S YOU,
SOMETHING I CAN'T GET ENOUGH OF.
IT TAKES ME ON A CRAZY ADRENALINE RUSH,
BUT I KNOW I CAN'T TOUCH,
AT LEAST I'M NOT SUPPOSED TO.

BUT HERE I AM, ONLY WANTING YOU TO TOUCH ME,
WHILE YOU GET TOUCHED ON BY EVERYONE BUT ME.
HOW CAN I SEE PAST THAT?
HOW CAN I NOT CONSTANTLY IMAGINE THAT?
NOT ALL THE THOUGHTS ARE GOOD ONES—
THEY'RE HEARTBREAKERS,
GUT-WRENCHING,
MEMORIES.

HOLDING THE WEIGHT OF MY HEART IN JUST ONE PICTURE,
KNOWING ONE DAY I'LL SCROLL PAST IT,
HOPING TO FORGET THAT YOU EVEN EXISTED.
BUT THAT HURTS MY HEART,
KNOWING I HAVE TO LEAVE BEHIND SOMEBODY I LOVED,
SOMEONE I TOOK THE TIME TO LEARN,
ALL FOR NOTHING
ALL FOR HEARTBREAK.

"BE SAFE OUT HERE,"
A PHRASE THAT ONCE BROUGHT ME COMFORT,
PRAYING FOR MY PROTECTION,
PRAYING THAT I COME BACK TO YOU.

SOMEWHERE IN OUR LOVE THAT NO LONGER EXISTED,
"BE SAFE OUT HERE"
BECAME GOODBYE.
A WORD EVERYONE IS SO FRIGHTENED TO USE—
GOODBYE.
A WORD SO POWERFUL,
IT BECOMES FINAL.
THE FINAL GOODBYE ALWAYS FOLLOW UP WITH
"BE SAFE OUT HERE."

WHAT IS IT LIKE TO BE IN LOVE?
TO BE IN LOVE IS A MAGICAL FEELING,
LIKE A FAIRY GODMOTHER BRINGING YOUR EVERY WISH
TO BE TRUE WITH A SINGLE BIBBIDI-BOBBIDI-BOO.
WHERE YOU CAN JUST STARE AT THEM FOR HOURS,
AND ENJOY EVERY IMPERFECTION THEY HAVE BECAUSE IT'S
PERFECT FOR YOU.
BEING IN LOVE IS A SURREAL FEELING THAT YOU WILL MAKE NO
MISTAKE TO *RECOGNIZE*,
A FEELING WITH NO DISGUISE.
UNLESS IT'S ABOUT THIS GUY I USED TO KNOW,
WHO HAD THE BEST MASK IN THE WORLD
TO MASK HIS TRUE INTENTIONS WITH ME.
BUT THAT'S WHEN YOU CAN TELL THE LOVE HAS FADED,
BECAUSE BEING IN LOVE IS ONE OF THE GREATEST FEELINGS—
A RELIEF KNOWING YOU HAVE YOUR PERSON,
STAYING AWAY FROM EVERYONE LIKE A BAD RUMOR,
DOING NOTHING TO JEOPARDIZE THIS LOVE.
A LOVE THAT MOST PEOPLE CRAVE, BUT DON'T KNOW WHAT TO
DO WITH IT.

RECIPROCATION

I'LL DO FOR YOU WHAT YOU DO FOR ME,
BUT THAT'LL NEVER BE ENOUGH,
ESPECIALLY FOR SOMEONE WHO DOESN'T FEEL
LIKE THEY'RE ENOUGH.
BUT I SEE THAT,
AND CONTINUE RECIPROCATING JUST FOR YOU,
JUST BECAUSE I LOVE YOU.
ALL I ASK FOR IS THAT YOU TREAT ME RIGHT IN
RETURN.

THE PERSON WHO BROKE YOU
WILL NOT BE THE PERSON TO HEAL YOU.

IT ALL MAKES SENSE,
IT COMES FULL THROTTLE,
A FULL PUNCH TO THE HEAD OF EVERYTHING I
ALREADY KNEW BUT WAS DUCKING AND DODGING.
WHY COULDN'T YOU JUST UNDERSTAND?
HE WASN'T MEANT FOR YOU.
HE STILL HAS YOUR HEART AS IF HE DOESN'T KNOW
WHAT TO DO WITH IT.
HE DROP-KICKS IT AND THEN ACTS CLUELESS.
BUT YOU'RE FOOLISH ENOUGH TO ALLOW IT,
AND BE OKAY WITH IT.

PUTTING THE BLAME ON EVERYONE BUT YOURSELF,
FOR LOOKING IN THE PAST WHEN THE PERFECT PERSON
RIGHT IN FRONT OF YOU.

I JUST WANT TO POUR MY HEART OUT AND LET YOU FIX IT,
TO REPAIR THAT DAMAGE THAT YOU INVENTED.
BECOME A SEAMSTRESS AND STITCH ME UP.
I JUST WANT TO CRY TO YOU ,
WHILE YOU FIX IT,
WIPE EVERY TEAR AND HOLD ME DEAR.

I KNOW I'M LIVING IN FEAR, STAYING WITH MY HURT,
BUT I LOVE YOU.
I TRULY HAVEN'T GOTTEN OVER YOU.
MY HEART FEELS HEAVY WHEN I HAVE TO MOURN YOU,
BUT YOU'RE NOT DEAD.
YOUR ALIVE, THRIVING, AND SUCCEEDING.
YOUR MAKING STRIDES, BUT HERE I AM,
COUNTING MY TIME ,
COUNTING HOW MANY DAYS WE'VE BEEN APART.

IT'S ALWAYS A CONSTANT BATTLE BETWEEN THE TWO—
WHETHER IT'S YOUR HEART AND MIND,
MIND VS. MOUTH,
YOU VS. YOU,
SETTLING OR COMPROMISING.
WE CAN NEVER JUST CO-EXIST.

OUR HEART AND MIND ARE THE WORST BATTLE.
WE SPEND HOURS FIDDLING WITH IT.

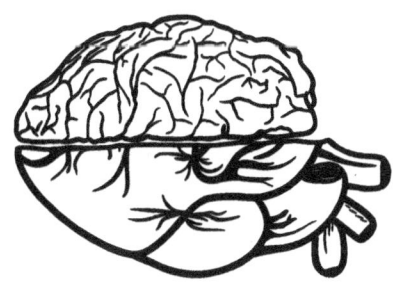

SOMETHING FEELS DIFFERENT—
A COMFORTING TYPE OF LOVE,
A STEADY LOVE,
A LOVE WHERE WE GROW OLD TOGETHER,
FINDING A DEEPER MEANING,
CRAVING THE POSSIBILITY
THAT WE COULD LOVE,
LOVE EACH OTHER LIKE NO ONE ELSE MATTERS,
GIVING EACH OTHER A PEACE OF MIND.
EVERY TIME I GIVE YOU A PIECE OF MINE,
A PIECE OF MY HEART THAT YOU LOVE AND NURTURE,
A PIECE OF ME THAT CAUGHT YOUR ATTENTION,
MAKING YOU WONDER,
"HOW CAN I HELP HER?"
THE QUESTION YOU MAY ASK YOURSELF OFTEN,
BUT WHEN YOU SAY IT TO ME,
IT JUST MAKES ME SOFTER.
IT MAKES ME MELT LIKE A SLUSHIE IN THE SCORCHING HOT SUMMER,
BECAUSE I ONLY THOUGHT A FEELING LIKE THIS
COULD COME FROM A NEW LOVE.

CONTINUED.

A FIRST-TIME LOVE,
A KID KIND OF LOVE,
WITH NO EVIL INTENTIONS,
BUT YOU'RE SHOWING ME A PURE LOVE,
AN INTENTIONAL LOVE,
A HAPPILY EVER AFTER LOVE,
WHERE YOU'RE MY PRINCE CHARMING,
WANTING TO COME SAVE ME—
SAVE ME WITH THAT ONE MAGICAL KISS,
THE ONE WE SHARE TOGETHER,
ONE BRINGING LOVE BACK TO LIFE,
GIVING EACH OTHER HOPE FOR A NEW LIFE.
A SOFT, GENTLE LOVE,
A HEALTHY, ROMANTIC LOVE,
AN EASY, NATURAL LOVE,
A SUNDAY-TYPE OF LOVE .
I'LL CONTINUE TO WAIT FOR YOU TO SAVE ME,
UNTIL THE DAY YOU SEE
I AM YOUR PRINCESS, WAITING TO NURTURE YOU,
STANDING BY YOUR SIDE,
YOUR RIDE OR DIE—
SOMETHING LIKE BONNIE AND CLYDE.
SOMEHOW, A LOVE LIKE THIS GETS FLIPPED,
AND ONE GETS LEFT IN THE DIRT.

CALM, COOL, AND COLLECTED,
IS WHAT I AM...
I COLLECTED ALL OF MY EMOTIONS AND FELT THEM.
YES, THEY WERE PAINFUL, BUT NOT FOR WHAT YOU THINK.
THE SWEETNESS HAS LEFT—
IT'S FAR FROM HONEY, WHICH THEY ONCE KNEW US AS.
AN ERA OF MINE THAT I HAD TO GRIEVE,
FOR A BIT OF FUN.

YOU'LL NEED A TIME MACHINE TO GO BACK,
TO WHEN YOU MADE THIS CHOICE
AND PUT THE BLAME ON ME,
DISREGARDING MY EMOTIONS.
I'M CALM TALKING TO YOU.
I'M WALKING AWAY CALMLY,
AND THAT MIGHT JUST BE THE MOST DANGEROUS WAY.
I'M NOT ANGRY, SAD, OR FURIOUS ANYMORE,
BUT YOU CAN'T GET YOUR WAY ANYMORE.
YOU DON'T HAVE THE SAME EFFECT ON ME.
I'M NOW CALM, COOL, AND COLLECTED.

THEN, SUDDENLY, I COULDN'T REMEMBER YOU ANYMORE.
YOUR VOICE SLOWLY DISAPPEARED.
THE MEMORIES WENT AWAY.
YOUR TOUCH NO LONGER EXISTED.
IN JUST A SHORT PERIOD, YOU'VE BEEN FORGOTTEN.

LETTING GO OF EVERYTHING IS HARDER THAN
EXPERIENCING THE HEARTBREAK ITSELF.

EVEN THOUGH I FELT SAFE WITH YOU PHYSICALLY,
MENTALLY, I'VE ALWAYS FOUGHT FOR MY SAFETY.

HERE I AM, FEELING EMPTY AGAIN,
BUT THIS TIME IT'S JUST BLANK.
MY EMOTIONS ARE NOW JUST AN EMPTY TANK,
THAT WAS ONCE SO FULL OF LIFE.
NOW, IT'S LIFELESS—
EMPTY.

YOU LEAD ME AWAY,
FAR, FAR AWAY FROM ME.
YOU LEFT ME STRANDED EVERY TIME I NEEDED YOU.
MY BIGGEST TAKEAWAY WAS HOW BADLY ME WANTING YOU
LEFT ME PATIENTLY WAITING FOR UNCONDITIONAL LOVE.
MY BIGGEST TAKEAWAY IS: I DON'T NEED YOU LIKE I THOUGHT I DID.

"BYE"
IS A FAREWELL BEFORE YOU LEAVE,
BUT I DIDN'T GET ONE.
YOU DIDN'T HAVE THE COURAGE TO BE
MAN ENOUGH TO SAY *BYE* FOR GOOD.

SORRY,
SOMETHING I'VE HEARD SO MUCH, IT'S LOST IT'S MEANING.
I'M SORRY—
WITHOUT ACTION, IT'S MANIPULATION.
SOMETHING I'VE FALLEN VICTIM TO MANY TIMES.
I WANTED TO BELIEVE YOU CARED,
CARED ABOUT ME AND MY FEELINGS.
NOW, IT WAS JUST A DELUSION—
THE DELUSION I WOULDN'T MIND GOING BACK TO AGAIN.

I CAN'T KEEP DEALING WITH THE SAME PAIN OF HEARING,
"I'M SORRY IT WON'T HAPPEN AGAIN."
NO LONGER HOLDS IT'S MEANING,
JUST FULL OF BROKEN PROMISES.

I REALLY JUST WANT TO BELIEVE,
BUT THEN I GOTTA SEE THINGS FOR WHAT IT IS:
YOU WEREN'T REALLY SORRY,
AND YOU DIDN'T REALLY CARE.
YOU JUST NEED TO SAY SOMETHING TO HOLD ME OVER,
SO YOU WOULDN'T HEAR MY TEARS.

WORDS SPEW FROM YOUR LIPS, MEANING NOTHING.
THEY FLOOD MY EARS, JUST TO SPILL OUT THE OTHER.
NOTHING YOU SAY STICKS ANYMORE.
YOUR BEHAVIOR MAKES YOU LOSE VALUE.
YOUR WORDS BECOME WORTHLESS—
SOON AFTER, YOU DO TOO.

I'VE COMPLETELY LET GO OF MY FEAR AND
BECAME RELAXED AT THE THOUGHT OF YOU.
MAYBE BECAUSE I'M COMFORTABLE AROUND
YOU,
MAYBE BECAUSE I FELT SAFE,
MAYBE BECAUSE I WAS CURIOUS—
IF I WOULD REJECT HIS TOUCH.

AT FIRST, I WAS HESITANT, PLAYING IT CRAZY.
I STOPPED HOLDING BACK,
NO LONGER FEELING GUILTY,
RIPPING THE BAND-AID OFF TO SEE THAT I'VE
FINALLY HEALED THAT SCAR.

MAYBE I SHOULD'VE TAKEN YOU SERIOUS
FROM THE START.
MAYBE WE WOULD'VE BEEN FAR.

THE ILLUSION
OF BEING OKAY WHEN YOU'RE NOT IS INCREDIBLE.
I NEVER KNEW HOW WELL YOU HAD TO WEAR YOUR MASK
UNTIL I STARTED WEARING MINE.
LETTING THE TEARS FLOW AND DROP, GOING UNNOTICED—
BEING IN A ROOM FULL OF PEOPLE,
WHILE THEY'RE HAPPILY BEING IN MY PRESENCE.
BY THE TIME IT'S UP, THE TEARS HAVE DISSOLVED
MY HEART GOING NUMB,
MY MIND SCREAMING, *WHY ME?*
AS MY THOUGHTS ARE SENDING PRAYERS TO GOD TO HELP ME,
TO GIVE ME THE STRENGTH I NEED.

EMOTIONS ARE JUST AN ILLUSION—
SOMETHING ONE MIGHT SEE, BUT THE NEXT MIGHT NOT.
A MASK WE THROW ON
TO GIVE A FALSE ILLUSION.

I DON'T HAVE TO STAND BY YOU
WHILE YOU WISH YOU WERE BY SOMEBODY ELSE.
I CAN DISAPPEAR WHENEVER I WANT TO.

I DON'T KNOW ANYMORE.
I THOUGHT I KNEW WHAT I WAS DOING,
TRYING TO PLAY A GAME OF TWO.
NOW I'M STUCK IN THE MIDDLE,
LISTENING TO MY HEART AND MY BRAIN—
NOT KNOWING WHAT TO DO,
LEAVING ME CLUELESS ON WHO TO CHOOSE,
OR IF I'M THE ONE TO EVENTUALLY LOSE.

I GAVE MY HEART TO HIM WITH NOTHING PUMPING LEFT.
HE GAINED CONTROL OF IT—
HE POSSESSED IT.
BUT NOW, I HAVE TO FIND A WAY TO *SNAKE* HIM TO GET IT BACK.

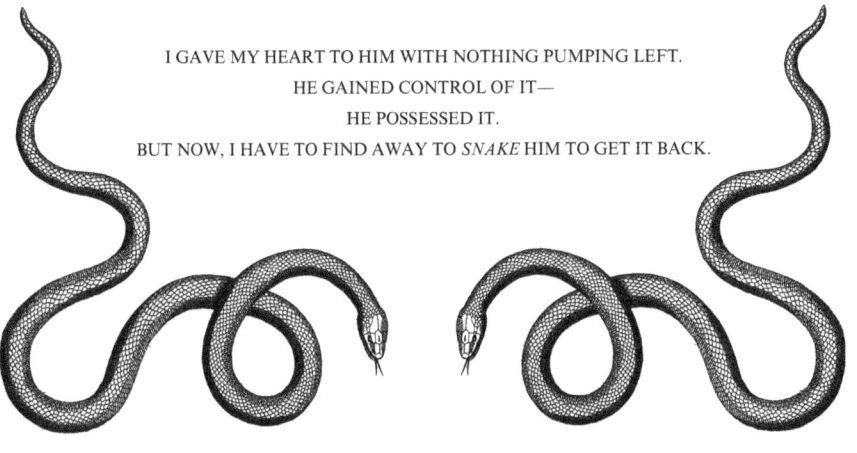

MEMORIES
ARE SOMETHING I NOW LIVE FOR,
A MEMORY OF ME AND YOU
SITTING IN THE CAR, VIBING TO MUSIC,
WITH MY THOUGHTS RACING AGAINST EACH OTHER.

ONE CAR REPRESENTING MY FEARS, WORRIES, AND DOUBTS,
WHILE THE OTHER CAR IS THE HAPPINESS AND JOY YOU BRING ME.
WITHIN INCHES, EVERY MINUTE COUNTS, AND THE SECOND CAR COMES UP
FOR THE WIN—
THE WIN FOR YOU TO GRAB THE KEY TO MY HEART AND UNLOCK IT.
AND YOU USE IT CAREFULLY,
KNOWING THAT I'M FRAGILE,
AND YOU DON'T WANT TO BREAK ME.

TO CREATE A MEMORY SO PASSIONATE THAT ALL I CAN DO IS REMINISCE
AND SIT,
IN THE VERY INSTANCE, FEELING EVERY FLUTTER WITH MY HEART
THAT I FELT IN THAT MOMENT—
THAT MOMENT OF BLISS,
FROM OUR VERY FIRST KISS,
WHICH, MIGHT I ADMIT, I TRIED TO FORGET
BUT COULDN'T.

THAT NEXT KISS FROM SOMEBODY ELSE MADE ME FEEL SICK,
BECAUSE IT WAS NEVER AS MAGICAL AS THE ONE I HAD WITH YOU.

BUT MAYBE IT WAS JUST THE LIQUOR
MAKING ME DO WHATEVER YOU SAY—
OFF THE DUESSÉ, AS BOTH WERE,
YET YOU STILL TOOK YOUR TIME WITH ME,
I WANTED TO SAY, *BLAME IT ON BEING UNDER THE INFLUENCE,*
BUT THAT WOULDN'T HAVE BEEN TRUE TO ME OR YOU.

EVEN AFTER THAT,
YOU'VE MADE ME CRAVE YOU IN A WAY NOBODY CAN REPLACE,
OR FILL THE VOID OF THIS HAPPY MEMORY—
THE MEMORY OF ME AND YOU TOGETHER,
REMINDS ME OF TWO KIDS DANCING IN THE RAIN,
GETTING SOAKED IN EMOTIONS,
WHILE OUR SKIN SOAKS EVERYTHING UP,
UNTIL WE GET IT THROUGH OUR HEADS TO MAKE THAT LOOK DIFFERENT.

BECAUSE WHEN WE'RE LIVING IN THE MOMENT,
WE CAN'T SEE HOW BEAUTIFUL OUR MOMENTS WERE
UNTIL IT BECAME A MEMORY.

YET, YOU STILL TOOK YOUR TIME WITH ME.

LATE NIGHTS,
STAYING UP ALL NIGHT TO TALK,
 WATCHING THE SUNSET AND RISE,
GETTING TO KNOW YOUR INNERMOST SECRETS,
LISTENING AND GIGGLING—
IS HOW I WANT MY LATE NIGHTS.

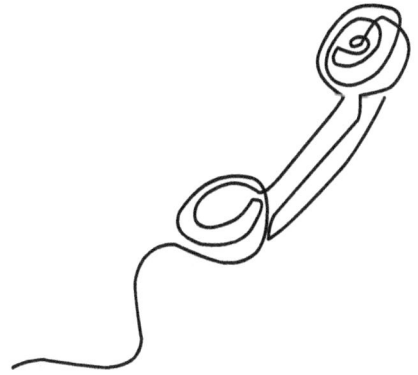

KNOWING WHEN TO LET GO CAN STOP—
THE PAIN,
THE DRAMA,
THE TOXICITY,
HEADACHES AND HEARTBREAKS.
KNOWING WHEN TO LET GO IS TRULY AN ART
THE ART OF DETACHMENT,
FINALLY LETTING GO TO CREATE A NEW PATH,
A PATH AWAY FROM YOUR PAST LIFE.

ON A HIGH,
YOU COULD'VE FOOLED ME WHEN I WAS HIGH OFF OF YOU.
SOMETHING I THOUGHT WAS EXTRAORDINARY BECAME ORDINARY—
TWO OF THE SAME.
THE EXACT THING I WAS RUNNING FROM,
YOU SO SMOOTHLY DISPLAYED.
MAYBE THAT'S WHY I'M HOLDING ON,
WHEN I KNOW I NEED TO LET GO.
I NEED TO JUST JUMP SHIP BEFORE I CRASH AGAIN.
IT FEELS LIKE MY HEART HAS BECOME AN ICEBERG,
AND IT'S IN THE MIDDLE OF AUSTRALIA, WITH SUMMER HEAT BLAZING ON ME—
WAITING FOR YOU TO COME TO YOUR SENSES TO RESCUE ME.

BUT YOU'RE NOT.

INSTEAD, YOU'LL THROW THINGS AT ME TO DISTRACT ME FROM THE REAL PROBLEM—
THE WAY YOU TREAT ME,
THE WAY YOU SEE ME,
THE WAY YOU DEAL WITH ME.

I THINK IT'S TIME FOR ME TO LET THE BOTH OF YOU GO,
SO YOU CAN ROAM FREE AND CHOOSE YOUR NEXT VICTIM,
AND LEAVE ME BE—
SO I WON'T HAVE TO SIT HERE IN DEFEAT AFTER EVERY INTERACTION WE HAVE,
AFTER BEGGING FOR SOMETHING THAT YOU COULDN'T GRASP.

BUT I COULDN'T GRASP THE FACT THAT NOBODY WHO LIKES AND LOVES YOU
WILL EVER HAVE YOU CONFUSED—
BUT WILL MAKE SURE YOU KNOW THAT YOU'RE THE *ONE* FOR THEM.

OUR LOVE WAS TESTED
BY DISTANCE—
ONE HUNDRED FIFTY MILES APART,
FORCED A LOVE SO INSEPARABLE
TO BREAK.

THE REALIZATION OF
IT'S ALL FAKE—
THE FEELINGS,
THE MEMORIES.
WE CREATED A FANTASY WITH PEOPLE WHO COULD CARELESS,
TO SEE WHO IS BETTER THAN THE NEXT,
WHO'S MORE HEALED THAN THE NEXT,
WE'RE ALL SECRETLY IN COMPETITION WITH SOMEONE,
TO BE CHOSEN—
BY THAT PERSON,
JOB, OR FAMILY,
WHEN THEY WANT NOTHING TO DO WITH YOU.
LOSING YOURSELF TRYING TO PROVE A POINT,
TO REALIZE THIS COMPETITION IS ALL IN YOUR HEAD
IS THE REAL WIN.

YOU DIDN'T TELL ME THE CONS OF BEING WITH ME,
YET YOU MIRRORED THEM SO PERFECTLY.

AFTER A FULL YEAR,
ITS TIME TO LET THE IDEA OF ME AND YOU GO.

SIMPLY JUST EXISTING,
THE PERFECT BACKGROUND CHARACTER
IN THE CHAOTIC PLACE CALLED EARTH.

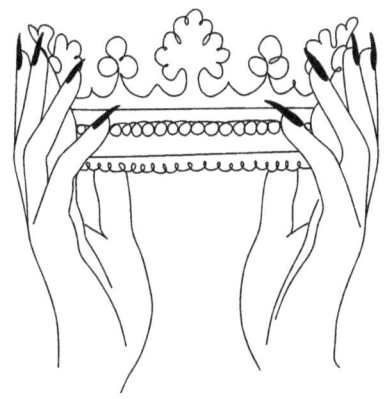

OUR FAIRYTALE,
ONCE UPON A TIME TO A HAPPILY EVER AFTER,
BUT AS QUICK AS IT STARTED, IT FINISHED,
LEAVING ME IN A FALSE ILLUSION.
YOU DESTROYED MY FANTASY WITH A BUNCH OF BROKEN PROMISES—
PROMISES I BELIEVED IN AND TRUSTED YOU WITH.

I WANTED TO FEEL LIKE THE QUEEN IN MY FAIRYTALE,
BUT YOU DIDN'T MAKE ME FEEL LIKE ONE.
I WAS MORE SO A SERVANT TO YOUR FANTASY,
ONCE APON A TIME, I WAS OKAY WITH IT.

I FELL TO YOUR KNEES AND FOLLOWED YOUR EVERY COMMAND,
EVERY DEMAND.
MY HAPPY ENDING WAS NOWHERE TO BE FOUND.
WAS I EVER YOUR QUEEN, OR WERE YOU PLAYING MAKE-BELIEVE?
WHERE I BELIEVED YOUR WORDS MORE THAN YOUR ACTIONS.
YOU WERE MY KING—WHY WOULDN'T I?
WHY WOULDN'T I NOT CATER TO YOU?

BUT THEN I REMEMBERED MY POWER,
THE POWER I WAS GIVING AWAY SO FREELY,
THE POWER I NEEDED TO BE THE QUEEN.
TAKE BACK MY THRONE, I RELUCTANTLY GAVE TO YOU.
AFTER ALL, I JUST WANT TO BE YOUR QUEEN,
THE QUEEN TO THE KING,
HAPPILY EVER AFTER.

I CAN STILL GET MY HAPPY ENDING ONCE I'M FINALLY OVER YOU

YOU WANT ME TO BE EVIL IN YOUR HEAD,
THE BAD MAN,
BUT IN REALITY, I JUST WANTED A REAL MAN—
A MAN TO PROTECT ME,
A MAN SO NURTURING
THAT YOU'LL NURSE ME BACK TO HEALTH.
A MAN THAT'S ATTENTIVE,
LOOKING SO DEEP INTO WHAT I SAY
HE ALREADY HAVE THE NEXT PLAY.
A MAN THAT'S GENTLE
TREATING ME AS IF I'M A MARSHMALLOW.

YOU WERE THOSE THINGS, BUT NEVER ALL TOGETHER.
YOU'VE HURT ME MORE THAN I WOULD'VE EVER THOUGHT.
AT LEAST IT STOPPED —
IT STOPPED WHEN I BECAME NOBODY TO YOU.

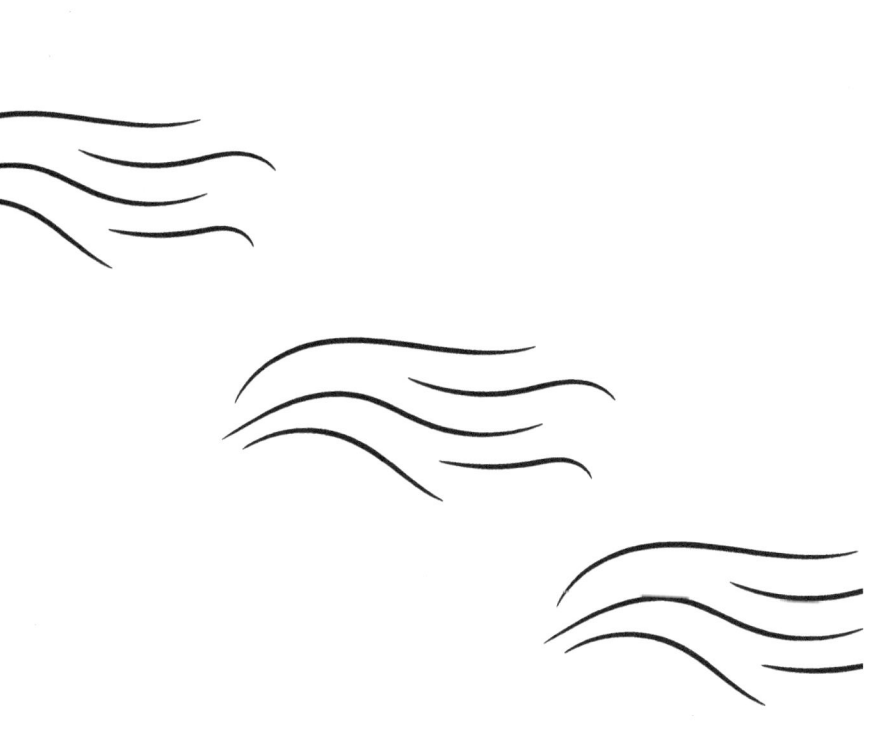

I THOUGHT I WOULD FINALLY BE ABLE TO BREATH.
BUT HERE I AM, CRYING SO HARD
I CAN BARELY BREATH.

YOU'VE GIVEN ME MY LAST HEADACHE.
I'M FINALLY WASHING MY HANDS WITH YOU—
NO MORE CONFUSION,
NO TEARS,
NO MORE WANTING TO BE THERE,
NO LONGER WANTING TO START ANOTHER SEASON WITH YOU.
I'VE COME TO THE FINALE OF OUR SERIES.

A FANTASY WE ALL LIVE FOR,
THE FEELING OF BEING WANTED,
MAKING IT HARD TO COMMIT.
TRULY, I JUST WANTED TO BE WANTED BY YOU,
BUT YOU COULDN'T FIGURE IT OUT.
YOU COULDN'T UNDERSTAND MY THEOLOGY OF THE FANTASY I CREATED.
YOU'VE MADE ME FEEL THIS WAY BEFORE, BUT NOT FOR LONG.
SO LET'S JUST TRY AGAIN—
ME, YOU, AND MY FANTASY.

I WAS THERE FOR YOU IN YOUR LOWEST MOMENTS,
EVEN WHEN I COULDN'T BE THERE FOR MYSELF,
TRYING TO PROVE MY UNDYING LOVE FOR YOU.
IVE BECOME FOOLISH, ASSUMING YOU WOULD BE THERE AT MY LOWEST.
YOU COULDN'T EVEN SEE HOW LOW I WAS,
LIKE A DRIED-UP POND IN THE SCORCHING HEAT.

YOU'VE ALWAYS LEFT ME TO FIGURE IT OUT,
ALWAYS LEAVING WHEN IT SEEMED CONVIENT FOR YOU.
SOME WOULD SAY YOU HAVE PERFECT TIMING.

JUST ME AND YOU,
TOGETHER AGAINST THE WORLD,
BUT THIS REALITY IS MINIMIZED
WHEN YOU TAKE THE WINDOW SEAT BACK HOME,
LEAVING ME ALL ALONE,
MAKING TIME GO BY SLOW.

EVERY MOMENT I'M NOT WITH YOU,
I'M THINKING ABOUT YOU ALL DAY AND NIGHT,
WAITING FOR TIME TO SPEED UP
'TILL I SEE YOU AGAIN.

TO FEEL THE WARM EMBRACE,
TO SEE THAT BEAUTIFUL, BRIGHT SMILE.
TO FEEL A SENSE OF PEACE AND CALMNESS IN YOUR ARMS,
LIKE YOU'RE PROTECTING ME FROM THE WORLD.

YOU'VE BECOME THE SHIELD
TO THE UNKNOWING PROBLEMS FIGHTING AGAINST ME,
BUT I KNOW I COULD'NT CARE LESS
WHEN IM WITH *YOU*.
THINGS HAVE CHANGED A BIT SINCE YOU'VE BEEN GONE…
I'VE BEEN CRAVING YOU MORE,
BUT IM TRYING TO FIGHT IT.

IN MY OWN WORLD,
SEEING WHAT COULD BE BEAUTIFUL BETWEEN ME AND YOU,
IF WE JUST ALLOWED IT.

WITHOUT ANYBODY KNOWING WHO'S IN THE PLANE,
BUT ME AND YOU.
NO DISTRACTIONS.

I'LL WAIT AROUND FOR YOU
LIKE AN EIGHT-YEAR-OLD WAITING TO SEE
WHAT SANTA BOUGHT THEM
AT EIGHT IN THE MORNING CHRISTMAS DAY,
EAGERLY JUMPING UP AND DOWN,
WAKING THE WHOLE HOUSE—
TO SEE WHAT WAS PATIENTLY WAITING
UNDERNEATH THE TREE.

YOU GIVE ME A FEELING
OF SOMETHING I'VE NEVER FELT BEFORE,
A GENUINE LOVE
WITHOUT ME HAVING TO DO ANYTHING.

I PRAY THAT IT'S A TRUE LOVE , NOT A LOOSE LOVE,
BECAUSE IT WOULD HURT TO LOSE YOU,
 BUT I IGNORED ALL THE CLUES.

ANYWAYS—
HERE WE GO, WASTING TIME,
SO IT CAN GO AHEAD AND PASS US BY,
STILL TRYNA FIGHT SOMETHING,
 WE CAN NO LONGER DENY.

SOMETHING GOD SET UP FOR US,
SOMETHING WE COULDN'T SEE WITH OUR OWN EYES,
SOMETHING SPECIAL THAT I PRAY WILL LAST.

BUT DON'T MAKE ME CONTINUE TO WAIT,
 LIVING WITHOUT YOU,
 BECAUSE TIME'S A-WASTIŃ.

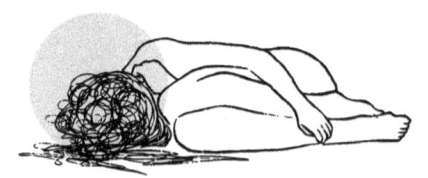

ALONE
IS WHAT I ENDED UP BEING AT THE END.
EVERY MORNING AND NIGHT—
ALONE.
SURROUNDED BY PEOPLE,
YET STILL ALONE.
A PERMANENT EMOTION,
OF FEELING EMPTY.

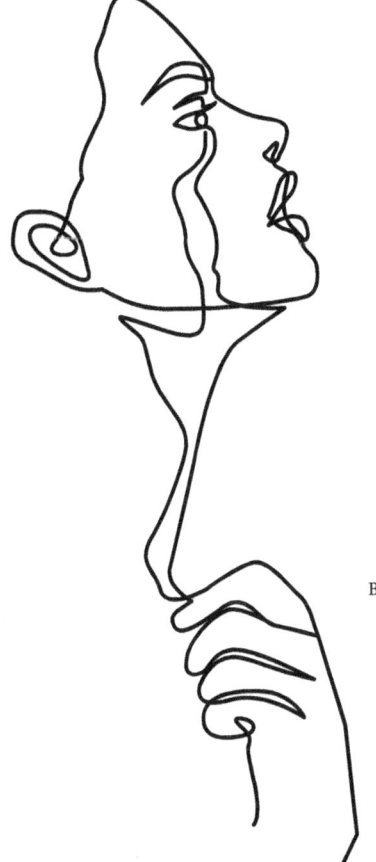

SOMETHINGS JUST CAN'T BE FIXED.
NOT ANYMORE.
THEY'VE LEFT YOU ALONE FOR TOO LONG
TO COME BACK AROUND.
DENYING YOU AS IF THEY NEVER KNEW YOU,
BACK ALONE WITH THE DRAINING THOUGHT OF
SOMEBODY NOT
CHOOSING YOU.

I WANT A LOVE LIKE PARADISE,
FOR YOUR VOICE TO BE THE BIRDS CHIRPING IN THE MORNING,
BEING THE FIRST THING I HEAR TO BRING A SMILE ONTO MY FACE,
SINGING A BEAUTIFUL, ANGELIC RHYTHM TO START MY DAY OFF WITH LOVE.

THE WIND SMOOTHLY MOVING AROUND ME,
TO KEEP ME COOL ON NIGHTS WHERE I FEEL LIKE IM GOING TO OVERHEAT,
ALLOWING MY BODY TO FOLLOW YOUR LEAD INTO WHEREVER YOU TAKE ME,
TO BRING ME THE SENSE OF PEACE I'VE BEEN LOOKING FOR,
WHERE YOU'RE SO STRONG,
BLOCKING EVERYTHING ELSE OUT SO IT'S JUST YOU AND ME.

A LOVE THAT FEELS LIKE THE SUN BURNING WITH SO MUCH PASSION,
YOU LEAVE A MARK,
A MARK THAT'LL MAKE ME SMILE AND REMIND ME OF THE GOOD TIMES
TOGETHER.
A LOVE THAT I'LL ADMIRE FOREVER,
TO KEEP ME BEATING AND WANTING MORE,
TO FEEL YOUR BODY ON MINE,
KNOWING OUR LOVE WILL NEVER DIE.

WALKING ON THE SAND, WITH EACH STEP LEAVING AN IMPRINT OF OUR LOVE,
AS WE APPROACH THE TRUE MEANING OF LOVE.

AS IF WE'RE THE OCEAN,
SOMETHING SO BEAUTIFUL IT'LL MAKE YOU CRY,
SOMETHING SO BEAUTIFUL NOBODY COULD EVER DENY,
THE SIGHT OF PEACE—
FEELING SO RELAXING IT LURES YOU WITH ONE WAVE AFTER ANOTHER,
GIVING YOU A COOL BREEZE TO BREATHE, TO CALM YOUR NERVES.
WITH EACH WAVE HITTING THE NEXT,
YOU TAKE A DEEP BREATH, WITH NO CARE IN THE WORLD IF THE WAVE COULD
SWEEP YOU AWAY,
BECAUSE YOU CRAVE WHAT PARADISE GIVES YOU—
THE TIDE, THE SAND IN BETWEEN YOUR FEET, THE SUNSET, THE FEELING OF LOVE.

I DON'T KNOW ABOUT YOU, BUT I WANT A PARADISE LOVE—
SOMETHING THAT IS NATURALLY IMPERFECTLY PERFECT,
A LOVE SO BEAUTIFUL NOBODY CAN DENY IT.

TO MY GIRLS,
THANK YOU FOR LISTENING TO MY CRIES,
AS WE BOTH EXPERIENCED OUR FIRST HEARTBREAKS TOGETHER.
LISTENING TO THE SOUND OF YOUR FRIEND BREAKING AND SINKING,
AS EACH DAY GOES BY,
LISTENING TO THE SAME STORY A MILLION TIMES.

THANK YOU FOR NEVER GETTING TIRED OF MY EMOTIONS

NEW BEGINNINGS
SOMETHING FRESH,
SOMETHING NEW AND RELAXED,
SOMETHING DIFFERENT.

THE BEGINNING OF A NEW JOURNEY—
A JOURNEY TO PROPERLY HEAL THE WOUNDS OF LAST YEAR.

LETTING THINGS GO AND MOVING ON.
CHEERS TO THE BEGINNING OF THREE HUNDRED SIXTY-FIVE DAYS!

IN CONCLUSION,
LOVE ISN'T WORTH YOUR MENTAL SANITY.

www.ingramcontent.com/pod-product-compliance
Lightning Source LLC
Chambersburg PA
CBHW022109090426
42743CB00008B/785